Marked by Fire

Marked by fire

Chosen to Make History

Patrea S. Brumfield

BE...BOLD

Marked By Fire
Copyright © 2020 by Patrea Brumfield

All rights reserved. Printed in the United States of America. No part of this book may be used or reproduced in any manner whatsoever without written permission except in the case of brief quotations embodied in critical articles or reviews.

For information contact :
Being Exceptionally...Beautiful.Optimistic. Limitless. Determined
PO BOX 870230
Stone Mountain, GA 30087
http://www.patreabrumfield.com

ISBN: 978-1-7352461-0-9

Table of Contents

MARKED BY FIRE

DEDICATION

INTRODUCTION

PART I - MARKED FOR PURPOSE

CHAPTER 1

CHAPTER 2

PART II - CHOSEN ONE

CHAPTER 3

CHAPTER 4

PART III - MARKED FOR HISTORY

CHAPTER 5

AFFIRMATIONS

ABOUT THE AUTHOR

ACKNOWLEDGEMENTS

BE B.O.L.D.

Dedication

I would like to first dedicate this book to the Great God that I serve. He is the One who ignites my FIRE. I would also like to dedicate this book to my husband William Brumfield, Jr., and my boys Jeremiah Brumfield and William Brumfield, III. Lastly, I dedicate this book to those who have been broken, hurt, misused, or misunderstood. To those who have made countless mistakes and feel as if there is no hope or no way out to rebound and recover. I'm here to tell you there is always a way out. God does not waste anything the good, the bad, or the indifferent. You can recover! You have been marked to bring someone else out! You have been Marked By FIRE.

Introduction

I don't think it's by chance that you are holding this book in your hands. I believe God divinely led you to this book to inspire you, empower you, and to challenge you to be everything that He has called you to be. You have been marked and set apart to do great and mighty exploits for the Kingdom of God.

It is up to us to advance the Kingdom of God and embrace who we are in Christ Jesus. In order for us to do that, we must accept who God created us to be. When God marks us, He challenges us. He challenges our thinking. He challenges our being. He challenges our belief systems. I believe this book will be just the right fit for you. It's time to start fires wherever you go, knowing that God has called and purposed you to do something greater than you could ever imagine on this Earth; in a unique, unorthodox, and in an authentic way. The time is NOW.

What are you waiting for? You have been hand-selected, chosen by the hand of the Master Creator. He has granted you access. Right now you may be thinking, "Patrea, you don't understand, I don't feel like I'm good enough. I don't feel like I have what it takes to do something amazing." Well, can I tell you this? Your feelings can't be trusted any! Now you may even say, "but Patrea, you don't understand! People will talk about me... they'll say I'm not qualified. People will say I am crazy. They are going to remind me of my past, and then what am I going to do then?"

This is what I will say to all of those excuses that maybe floating around in your head right at this moment. "Maybe so... so what? Let 'em talk, talk is cheap!Let 'em watch you grow and elevate! Let 'em see the glory of God moving in your life and in the lives of those you touch. What others have to say... doesn't matter. It is God's desire that you discover who He has truly designed, crafted, and created you to be." With that being said...IT'S TIME TO STEP OUT!

As you read through the pages of this book, I pray that you hear the voice of the Lord and feel His gentle tugs on your heart strings. God does not want us to remain in bondage. He does not want us walking around clueless and confused about who we are. He does not want us to be downtrodden or broken. God wants us to be whole!

God already knows the mistakes that we are going to make, and the victories we will win! As a matter of fact, He knows all of this before these instances ever happen! So, keep pressings forward!

As you will see within the pages of this book are my shared personal thoughts, beliefs, and perspectives. I bare all by sharing my personal experiences and my battle with depression, rejection, perfectionism, fear, shame, and bitterness—and how God brought me out of them all! As I always say, "there is nothing in me that makes me great, but the One who lives in me that makes me great." He marked me with His Fire. He chose me for His purpose, and I'm so honored that He did.

My Prayer for you:
> *Dear Heavenly Father, I thank You for the one that's holding this book in their hands. I pray that You expose every area where the enemy tries to hide, squat, or crouch. I pray that You will bring liberty, peace, joy, comfort, understanding, and revelation of who You purposed them to be. I thank You for revealing their purpose; enabling them to grab hold to it and walk in it with authenticity, boldness, courage, and faith. God, You did not give them the spirit of fear; but power, love, and sound mind. You marked them with a purpose and set them apart for such a time as this. Lord, I ask that You break down every wall. Expose any and everything that will try to halt their progress, stunt their growth, and rob them of their destiny. Lord, I thank You in advance for their freedom now. In the name of Jesus Christ, amen.*

If you made this far, that means you are ready to embrace your mark. I'm super excited to share my experiences and thoughts with you. I hope that you will find peace on your journey as you read about my highs and my lows; my victories and defeat; and how I managed to overcome.

I pray that something will be said between the pages of this book that will cause you to grow, thrive, and develop into the person God predestinated you to be despite opposition. This book is broken up into three parts, and each section provides as a stepping-stone for breaking into your true identity; marked, equipped, and chosen.

Make yourself comfortable before you begin reading. Go

brew you a nice hot cup of tea, grab your favorite blanket, and find a cozy place to relax and dive right on in. It's going to be a journey...

PART I
MARKED FOR PURPOSE

Chapter 1

Marked

"You have been set apart as holy to the Lord your God, and he has chosen you from all the nations of the earth to be his own special treasure." Deuteronomy 14:2 (NLT)[1]

When we hear the term "marked" we somehow think right away it's an amazing thing—it is...but that amazing thing will cost us. I know we would like to close our eyes and wish ourselves into a paradise of great fortune without a cost but believe me...everything comes with a cost even when we are unaware of the price. Let me tell you, I struggled with this reality for years. I even questioned God, "why me?"

His response, "why not you?"

You see, we have all been created with purpose and for purpose. We all have been given a story and a journey. There is no other person who could ever sound like you, look like you, or do what you could do. We do not realize this of course until we reached a level of awareness and maturity. Before you and I were born, God designed us for a special assignment and purpose. God knew why He created you. He created you to be a powerful influence in the earth realm. He marked you to be the solution to a problem. However, we do not get to pick and choose the problems that we are to solve, or what process we have to go through; nor do we choose the path in which we are given.

So, I'll be a brave soul and will lay it all on the table by using myself as an example. Maybe you can learn from my mistakes, be encouraged from my victories, relate to my pain, or identify with some or all of my experiences. Either way, my desire is for you to understand the greatness that resides inside of you. I also want you to understand we all have a story to tell, and a past that we all sometimes just want to erase. But, I have found that everything in my past was necessary and needed for where God has brought me today. So here's my story...

Growing up, I was kinda' sorta' awkward; you know? I was that one girl who could never really fit in. I was an acquired and peculiar taste. I didn't really fit in; especially at school. The popular crew was overrated. I was...well, the in the not-so-popular crew. Back then, I considered myself basic, ordinary, common; a misfit if you will. I was that girl caught up in the twists and struggles of identity conflict from a very young age.

I didn't know where to fit or where to belong. It felt as if life had no real place for me. Like, really? Even within my family dynamics. It seemed like I was outed as a young girl. I was stereotyped and ostracized. People called me names and gave me labels such as bae-bae kid (a very bad child) or fast (attention-seeking from boys); and I was treated as such. I would act out because those words cut deep. My method was to do whatever I needed to masque the pain. But oh, on the inside...I was breaking, hurting, and embarrassed.

Now, what did that look like for a young girl who was already struggling with understanding herself, her identity, how unpretty she felt, and dealing with the feels of not being wanted? It was a heavy load to carry!   There was no hope. I was already deemed the "bad child", so who in the world would want me around?

So everything that I did came out looking and sounding like rebellion, anger, mischief, and disobedience. If you could name it, I was displaying it. My childhood identity was a constant struggle. When it came to attending school and dealing with non-family members, I tried my best to just fit in, belong, and feel like I was a part of something.

I tried to hang out with the black girls, the white girls, the Hispanic girls, the tough girls, the cute girls, the hot girls, the smart girls, the gossipy girls, the nice girls, the polished girls, and the messy-messy ghetto girls. To my surprise, every group I attempted to be a part of ended in an epic fail. I still couldn't find my place to fit. I occasionally found acquaintances, and we would occasionally speak, hang out for a season, but no real true loyalty or true friendship would become of them.

I tried to do everything I could do to be accepted or just to be apart, but with every attempt, failure was as close as my next breath. Just when I thought I found the right crew something would go awry. For a cool moment everything seemed to be heading in the right direction, and then, BOOM. Everything would go up in smoke. Other times the connection would just simply dissipate with no rhyme or reason. It just ended.

I went through this vicious cycle often. There were times where I was good, but not good enough. Cute, but not cute enough. Sweet, but just sweet enough to be mistreated, and gullible enough to be misused. I had nothing and felt like nothing. After a while, I just went out on a limb and tried to be everything rolled into one. I adopted all the clichés and mimicked all the trends. I know now that I was just fighting for a space in what seemed to be a world of impossibilities. I just needed something that would fill the void in the life that I saw as small and minuscule.

From grade school to high school, life for me became

more complicated; especially battling with identity issues, insecurities, doubts, fears, boyfriends, failed friendships; and let's not forget about that big awkward space of not belonging. Rejection wrapped around me like a cloak. I was surrounded by it. My relationships were driven by it. No matter where I went that spirit was not too far behind. I'm sure you can relate in some capacity. If you can't then just bear with me a few pages, I'm going somewhere with all of this.

To the naked eye of this young insecure girl, and what had been painted on the window of her mind concerning who she was, who she could be, and what she would possibly become was far-fetched. All I perceived about life; was ultimately doom. Life for Patrea was no fairy tale and had no good ending. There was no future for me. All I had was a whole pile of nothingness and exclusion.

Oh, but as life went on, and growth and maturity took its course, I was provided another chance, another reality! When the opprotunity came knocking to run into the arms of Jesus. I did! That's when things began to turn in the other direction. It took some time, but life began to look up for me. Now as an adult, and as a daughter of the King. I look through the lens and scope of my Heavenly Father, I can now see the handprint of God in it all. He uses it all!

Now, I understand that I wasn't created to fit in, instead, I was built to stand out. I wasn't made to blend in with the crowd. I was purposed to be set apart. I was strange for a reason. I was rejected for a reason. The rejection was necessary so that I wouldn't settle! The rejection revealed that God had something greater waiting for me. What He had for me was better! What He had was for me was something spectacular, something unique, and special just for me. I was a misfit for a reason. Sounds crazy right? But you'll come to understand as you go through the chapters ahead.

You see, my mom's absence from my life when I was a little girl wasn't meant to break me. Being raised by a single father didn't mean I was lacking. No! It was just an indication that I was marked and set apart to be an answer for people who could relate to me. So, yes! I was singled out! But, I was also hand-selected, appointed, and anointed to help others break into their destiny, embrace the good, bad, and ugly of their own journey; and to show others that God will use all the pieces of their story to encourage the heart of another! So, Yes! God marked me. He sat me aside for a purpose. He was reserving me for a set time, even when I couldn't understand it. Even when I couldn't see it! He considered me! He had a plan for me!

God was covering me. Even when I felt alone, He was with me, sustaining me. Even when I was being tricked and bamboozled by the enemy, I was being groomed and molded by the hand of God to do something extraordinary for Him on this Earth. If you think about it long enough—you'll find that you were too!

Now, does that mean I was absent of mistakes, failures, or excluded from trouble? Absolutely not! However, I am grateful and I do praise God for gracing me. God's love saved me, His grace rescued me, and by His blood He redeemed me. God distinctively marked me, and there is no denying it. Before I was born; he chose me. Before my heartbeat could be seen blinking on the monitor screen; God marked me. God marked you as well! Yes! To do something amazing right here and right now!

So, at this moment, I give you permission to let it go. All the disappointments, all the regrets, all the *Why Me's*, and all the shoulda', coulda', and woulda's. I release you to embrace your MARK OF GOD. You are His special treasure set apart for the Master's use!

You see, the enemy knew who we were purpose to be in the beginning. That's why he tries early on to destroy us! He knew and still knows just how powerful we really are. So, in his desperate attempts of trying to slaughter us early on by distorting the true vision and version of who we were meant to be was his goal, but his plans will never supersede God's plan for our lives. Now...I'm not saying that some of those assaults, tactics, and schemes didn't wound or diminish our souls, misconstrued our perspectives, or had an affect on our belief systems along the way. Tuh, I still battle with some issues myself. However, I'm fully persuaded that God has chosen you and me for something exceptional. Despite the issues...

Listen, you may or may not have felt like you didn't fit in. You may not have been in the popular crew at school, in the popular mom's or dad's club in the workplace, or on the powerful women's or men's ministry team. Tuh, you may or may not have ever had the opportunity to attend college or finished school in general. You may not have ever been the choicest of your family members. You may or may not have ever been accepted by your peers. You may or may not still to this day feel the same way. It's okay...

If you do still feel this way?. Good. That's a good thing. I know what you're thinking...how can this be a good thing, right? Let me que you in. Are you ready? You're not supposed to fit in when you were created to stand out! If you are in the valley of decision, and still struggle with this reality. Then can I tell you that you are in a good place to discover who you really are, and what you are really made of. You have been chosen. You have been MARKED BY FIRE!

There are certain types of people who God created to be drawn to you, they look like you, they can identify with you, they sound like you, they understand you, and they think like you. All for the purpose of understanding what and who they are made of! Giving you the opprotunity to connect them to purpose. Thus, advancing the Kingdom of God. When I say 'look like' I'm saying have the same interest, have similar experiencs, and drawn to the same things as you.

It's until you see things beyond the pain, frustration, or loneliness; and understand that you were marked to be an answer. Yep, YOU. You with all your imperfections. You with all your stuff. Yes, YOU. God uses it all. God doesn't make any mistakes, nor did He change His mind concerning you. He already knew your victories and defeat. Honey, accept it, and be thankful because of it! God marked you!

"For You formed my inward parts; You covered me in my mother's womb."[2]

"Your hands have made me and fashioned me; give me understanding to learn Your commandments."[3]

What Does It Mean to Be Marked?

According to Webster's dictionary to be marked means having an identifying mark or having a distinctive or emphasized character.[4] Another dictionary describes it as having a visible mark clearly noticeable and evident. [5] So in a nutshell... when God marks us, there is a discrete, apparent, and unquestionable indication that His hand is on us. Simply put, when you are marked—you to sound different, look different, and act different. You are DIFFERENT. You are distinguished... heads above the rest. Your anointing singles you out! Your authenticity calls you out! Your purpose pulls you out into the forefront! It was by God's design!

To be marked means that God—Himself selected you specifically and purposfully. It means that He has put something special on the inside of you that only you can do because you were created to do it. Ultimately, establishing and displaying God's glory in your life.

Now, that doesn't mean you are better than or greater than anyone else, because the truth of the matter is, we are all someone special to God and loved by God. However, Matthew 22:14 makes it clear that several will be called, but few will be chosen. I look at it this way: Some of us are not chosen to be singers, cooks, builders, seamstresses, truck drivers, bakers... but many are. And, it's totally fine if we are not in those categories.

Let's look at it from this viewpoint. Have you ever gone into a store to get some items for dinner, or maybe to grab some materials for a project? Well, while you're in the store you look over each item to see if whatever you are looking for is a good fit. You make sure that it isn't expired. You look for which brand would be best. You look at the size of the item, you investigate how it looks, you may even check how the item smell, or you may check the color scheme to see if it would be best for preparation. You carefully select which items will be used for the purpose and outcome of the dinner or project. That means you had to carefully consider what would be chosen. Right? You had to choose what would be beneficial for you. All items in the store had a purpose, had value and could get the job done, but many items were there, but were not all chosen. The items you chose were marked for a speific purpose. So, when we are marked by God, we are chosen. That's just that, and we have to embrace who we are.

Embracing Who You Are

When you hear the term "embrace who you are"? What comes to mind? No, really think about for a second? Often when we hear this term, some grapple over the concept, some grasp the concept, and others gloss right over it; as though they've already embraced who they really are, but could it be true? How would you know? This was a question that was deep-seated on the inside of me while attending the first Awakening Reloaded evening service. As I sat there in anticipation of what God would do during this amazing time of sisters gathering together. A small voice interrupted the intriguing thoughts of excitement racing through my mind. "Patrea, who are you?" I tried to ignore it, but throughout the service, this question continued to try to initiate a debate between my outer appearance and internal appearance. Frankly, I didn't want to be involved, but there was no escaping the demand of that still small voice. My initial thought was to just go to the altar call and repent when that invitation was granted, and that should make me feel better. Maybe this was the solution to the riddling question on repeat in my head. Right? Wrong!

Once I made my way down the aisles where everyone gathered for prayer. This persistent small voice was back...questioning my identity, testing my reality, and expose my vulnerability. I tried my best to dodge the confrontation with the still small voice forcing me to come to grips with the truth of my reality. As I stood at the altar the Holy Spirit came for the weakest part of me...my identity. Why were we back here? I had everything under control. I finally looked the part, and I finally found a way to hide all my inadequacies and imperfections behind my gifts, talents, and abilities. People seemed to like me now. I was included now.

As I stood there helpless and exposed, the Holy Spirit asked me again, "Patrea" who are you? I wanted to respond. I really did, but the truth of the matter was that I couldn't. I had gotten so wrapped up in who I believed I was, and who other people believed me to be that I couldn't recognize the truth of who I truly was myself? I was a FRAUD!

You see, God has a way of exposing what's broken and distorted in our perception of who we believe we are, exposing the underlying issues of our damaged our souls. Whether we like it or not.

This encounter that I'm speaking of came the night before I had to host our church's monthly Sisters With A Purpose

(S.W.A.P) meeting. I had everything planned to precision, and it was going to be awesome, but this encounter with the Holy Spirit stopped me in my tracks forcing me to look at things differently. I didn't sleep well, and I had about 16 hours left before I had a house full of women ready to hear what I would be teaching. And there I was... having second thoughts about everything, wondering if what I initially planned to teach would be beneficial or not. This question from the Holy Spirit hit me at my core. It was like pulling a loose string from a piece of fabric and watching it unravel.

Talk about a dilemma. I sat on my bed with a blank stare, with this question from the Holy Spirit rolling over in my head. "Patrea, who are you?"

It tore me apart with each proposal. Finally, I was completely and totally honest with myself, and I openly admitted to the Holy Spirit that I had no clue of who I was anymore. I kept repeating *I don't know, I don't know*. For a moment I was flooded with a variety emotions: anger, bitterness, frustration, guilt, shame, excitement, bewilderment, and relief. The emotional carousel continued until I simply surrendered to the truth of my current state of identity. I'm thankful that the Holy Spirit loved me enough to stop me in my tracks to confront me. After being made aware of my desperate need for His guidance; I was able to give God something to work with. Listen, we have to give God something to work with!

That night as I sat on my bed, the Holy Spirit began to pour into me the revelation about my true identity that can only be found in Christ. I started to launch my investigation and began to research scripture. I had to know who I was. I had to know what God had to say about me. For years I had lived out this faulty truth about me, it was the only truth I knew. That faulty truth was the only thing I had that identified me, and the only substance I knew to embrace...it was the "I am who I am" kinda' truth. Don't side-eye me because you know what I'm talking about. (This is just the way I am) You know...

For instance, I embraced rejection as my identity. It wasn't something that happen to me— it was me. Fear was my identity—inadequacy as my identity. Everything opposite of who and what God declared that I was—the lies became my truth. But, that night...the gig was up. The Holy Spirit began to pull back the curtain of shame, lack of self-esteem that had morphed into false confidence, and a pretense that gracefully covered the little girl who was never brave enough to step into who God created her to be.

Right there in my bedroom, the Holy Spirit stripped me of every false belief and false identity that I made as a permanent fixture in my life. The Holy Spirit brought to my remembrance a prior conversation with my husband years prior. It was almost as if my husband's words searched me out! Each word rang loud and clear in my spirit, "Patrea if you expose the enemy; the enemy can longer hold you."

I still hold fast to that truth. Once you expose the lie that the enemy has told. He has no where to hide so he has to let you go! Exposure will cause the enemy to back off!

As the time approached to expose it all, my heart raced. Lord, did I have to expose it all? Oh, geez...what would everyone say? What would they think of me? Back and forth the questions toggled through my mind, but I was amped up and ready to share the unmitigated truth of what the Holy Spirit revealed to me. I was ready to share MY truth. The REAL truth.

Have you ever been in a place where you've been confronted with the truth? Or have you ever just decided to ignore the pulling of the Holy Spirit and tried to regroup as best as you could? It's in those moments that we either agree with the truth, or we shrink and sink.

If we don't agree with what's being revealed to us; we

shrink back and continue to pretend, or we just give up and sink into depression or denial. That night I had a decision to make. Either I was going to continue being fake and phony or I was going to embrace my God-given identity. Whenever your confrontation comes, please choose God's way. Don't forfeit your birthright to just live a life of pretenses. That's what our enemy (satan) wants.

That night, I finally decided to do it God's way. I had to start from scratch. God challenged me in my identity, so I wanted my lesson to follow suit. I decided on the topic "Ordinary or Extraordinary: Which One are You?" This question was up close and personal, and it would pull on the heart of any person asked. God wanted to get us back into our proper position and operating from our true identities.

As I prepared, I placed both category titles on each side of the wall in the seating area. One by one each as each lady walked in, I would simply ask them if they deemed themselves as ordinary or extraordinary. Once they revealed their answer, I told them where they should be seated. You would've been amazed at how quickly the ordinary categorized side of the room filled. It still amazes me that most of the women who felt they were ordinary still supersede that category even to this day!

The lies that we believe are crazy. So, let me ask you a few questions. Who are you? What are some of the lies that you hear when asked this question? What's etched in your silent thoughts? What lies have robbed you of God's truth? Come on, think about it. Think about all the lies that have jaded your perception of who God truly created and called you to be. So again, I propose these questions: who are you, what are you made of, and what's your identity?

When we embrace who we truly are, our faith is increased, and we will walk in power knowing that we were "fearfully and wonderfully made" (Psalm 139:14).[6] The old us was crucified with Christ. There should be no reference point to turn back to, because we're reminded by 2 Corinthians 5:7 that "who so ever be in Christ is a new creation; old things have passed away, behold, all things are become new."[7] If you are a born-again believer then this truth pertains to you.

Our old habits, old behaviors, poor decisions made, bad relationships, and whatever else that was "Pre" salvation, (acceptance of the Lordship of Jesus Christ) has been written off. Our old identity no longer applies to us. That's enough to shout and praise God about. We serve a God that does not hold the past against us. However, the process is not as easy as it sounds. When we give our lives over to Christ and receive Him as Lord our spirits are free and perfect, but our souls—our souls have holes needing attention and work. We must allow God to reveal the things we've permitted to enter into our souls and come out of agreement with whatever He reveals!

Breaking into the true identity of Christ comes with work, because we have been born into sin, and shapen into iniquity (Psalm 51:5). We all have soul issues and there is no way around it except through the receiving Jesus as Lord over our lives (salvation), the blood of Jesus Christ, and through the truth of God's Word. You see, our minds have been conditioned to adapt to whatever is sinful. From birth, it is easier for us to fall into the pitfalls and cycles of sin, and into the lies of the enemy which detour us from being the true version God intended us to be. That's why the enemy doesn't want us to come into the full understanding of our God intended purpose because we pose a threat to the kingdom of darkness. As a matter of fact, it's because of who we are, and who we're connect it to…that WE ARE DANGEROUS to the kingdom of darkness.

I'm telling you all of this, because I don't want you going through the long hard struggling path of self-discovery; when you can learn from someone who has walked the path before you. Learn and take it from me. If you are going to walk in your God-given identity, you must abandon and renounce any image of yourself that is not from God. You must be selective about accepting what others have said about you, and even what you have said or still say about yourself. You must destroy every label that has ever been assigned to you. Even the labels you have assigned to yourself. If it's not God's truth—it doesn't belong to you.

We must come out of agreement with how people, and society define us. We must embrace who we really are according to the truth of God. Period. There is no other way around it. We must also be willing to destroy the belief system programmed from birth. So, how do we do that?

We must search out the scriptures and start researching what God says about us and what He has given to us. Start with the book of Ephesians. You will find out how blessed you are, and how God is pleased with how he created and designed you to be. Let the Word of God define you and let Him impress upon your heart your God-ordain purpose. Your feelings, your past, your accomplishments, the shape of your body, or how pretty or handsome you are does not determine who you are! You're not defined by the opinions of people, your boss, your successes, or failures, nor by your current circumstances. However, these things can shape our perception of who we think we should be, but we have the power to choose. You are defined by God and God alone.

He is Creator. He is Counselor. He knows our beginning and He knows our ending; even our in-between. He's God. He's Alpha and Omega, the Beginning and the End, the First and the Last. He's the All-Knowing One. The Omnipotent One. The Omniscient One. He's all-powerful. He's God, our Father; and with His hands, you and I were meticulously, methodically, intimately, and intently designed with PURPOSE. You are not here by mistake. God identifies you as being sealed with promise, established, and anointed by Him. *"Now He who establishes us with you in Christ and has anointed us is God, who also has sealed us and given us the Spirit in our hearts as a guarantee"* (2 Corinthians 1:21-22).[8]

Isn't that amazing!? He gives us the Holy Spirit as a guarantee.

According to Merriam Webster, to guarantee means "to undertake to answer for the debt, default, or miscarriage of; to engage for the existence, permanence, or nature of: undertake to do or secure; to give security to guarantee against loss, or to assert confidently. The death and resurrection of Jesus Christ sealed our fate, changed our identity, and secured our debt. So, how in the world could we ever identify with all that other stuff? When we accepted the Lord Jesus Christ, we became something exceptionally extraordinary. We were MARKED!

Chapter 2

Unmasking and Disarming

"The thief does not come except to steal, and to kill, and to destroy." John 10:10a (NKVJ)[9]

When you are marked to do something extraordinary for God, not only do you need to know who you are, but you need to be comfortable with exposing what you are not. Throughout the years I learned that I was marked to do great things for the Kingdom of God. I didn't know that demonic assignments, ambushes, ploys, plots, tricks, and attacks were setup to destroy me. The Bible tells us not to be ignorant of the devices of the devil. *"Lest Satan should take advantage of us; for we are not ignorant of his devices* (2 Corinthians 2:11 NKJV).

We are not only marked by fire, but we are targets as well. The devil knows that if he can convince us into believing his lies and come into agreement with them; then he has the opportunity to kill the seed of purpose within us. Even if you find yourself right now in a battle with these opposing lies stand your ground anyway.

Fight back anyway! Even if you don't fully understand the fight itself! Stand your GROUND, and don't give up or give in! Each time that you expose an area of weakness that requires healing and deliverance, another level of freedom is released to you. For every lie that you expose, the more victory you will have over it. Stand your ground! I'm going to say this before we delve into this chapter. Deliverance and healing is a process. Being able to recognize the roots and triggers is a process, and we cannot do this without the assistance of the Holy Spirit, trusted family, or friends. Exposing and uncovering things causes vulnerability, and at times can bring shame. So, connect with someone trustworthy during this process.

In this chapter, we will be unmasking and disarming demonic spirits and exposing their manifestations and operations. I have listed a few demonic influences that I believe will arrest the development of a believer. I personally believe that consistent moments of deliverance and healing from demonic strongholds are essential to our wellbeing and life as a Christian believer. Deliverance and healing are the children's bread.[10] God has given us the power to dispel darkness, and power to destroy the bands of wickedness. There is no reason that we should walk around tormented, depressed, vexed, and driven by demonic influences.

Let me make this plain. As a believer, we cannot be possessed. Possession is ownership. Demonic spirits are not owners of our souls, Jesus Christ is the owner and lover of our souls, and He purchased our souls with His blood. However, demonic spirits can oppress our souls. Oppression is described as, "prolonged cruel or unjust treatment or control."[11]

Nevertheless, the only power that any demonic force has against us is the power that we surrender. As we go through this chapter, I ask that you pray and ask the Holy Spirit to illuminate any area of your life where bondage or oppression from any demonic spirit that may have you bound.

As aforementioned in chapter one, it is imperative that we expose the enemy and every device that he hurls at us. Remember, when we expose the enemy, he can no longer hold us captive. The enemy won't be able to continue to keep you in a place of bondage. He can't harass, torment, or oppress you if you expose and disarm him. His goal is to try to keep us demobilized by ensnaring us and keeping us from operating and reaching our full potential so that we will forfeit the assignment on our lives.

I believe we have entered the season of "If it isn't God... Everything has to go". God is exposing in this season. He is exposing the true hearts of the believers, those who are in leadership, those who occupy prestigious positions in politics, ministries, governments, judicial system, educational system, and in our economical system. God is exposing us all. Nothing is off-limits.

My prayer is that as you continue to read, that the Spirit of the Lord would unmask and uncover every spirit that's not of God. May God uncover and expose the spirit of rejection, depression, fear, frustration, irritation, insecurity, control, bitterness, root of bitterness, manipulation, rebellion, anger, deception, and disappointment. All of it. I pray that all demonic influences, suggestions, and strongholds to be broken off your life. In the name of Jesus Christ. I plead, apply, and activate the blood of Jesus Christ over your mind, heart, soul, and spirit now in the name of Jesus Christ.

I ask that the Holy Spirit go down deep, exposing all that would keep the true you buried, crippled, stagnate, bound, and underdeveloped. For this reason, the Son of God was manifested, that He might destroy the works of the devil.[12] It's time to expose and unmask the ensnarement of the enemies within. In the name of Jesus Christ.

LET'S GET TO WORK.

Unmasking Rejection

"God please just take this emptiness away. I'm trying to love the best way I know-how. I'm trying to give what I don't have to give. I'm depleted. My good is just not good enough. I'm lonely, and I hate the fact that I have to endure this alone. You said that you would never leave me, so why do I feel this way."

This was one of the hard conversations I had with the

Lord. I found myself pleading with God in this way so many times. As I look back over those moments of my life pleading with God, I could plainly hear the shrieking screams coming from the pit of my burning throat. Oh, the misery, anguish, and uncertainty of it all. I often wondered if I should even keep going because I desperately wanted to give up in despair. I struggled in this place for years. I just wanted to be accepted and loved with no strings attached, no price tags... just me...not me always doing something to earn it... just simply accepted as ME. With all of my imperfections, my beauty, my triumphs, and my failures. All of me as I've allowed everyone else to be. Can you relate to this feeling?

I needed to understand why it was so hard for me. Why didn't I feel or receive the acceptance that I sought out? Well, if you can remember in the first chapter, I revealed that my mother was not present. I think that this void caused some friction with my reaility and expectations of others. I first met my mother when I was in the first grade. I was in love. Infatuated by her beauty, and hypnotized by her smile. I was head overhills for her. Where had she been all my life. The time spent with her was short lived. Like a thief in the night she was gone! She took my heart away, and left me feeling empty. The heartache seemed unbearable.

For years, I continued harboring feelings of abandonment. I never wanted her to leave my life. I longed for her presence when she was away, and after a year or two she resurface for awhile, and like vapor she was gone again. I thought was it something I did which caused her to leave. She was gone with no explanation. She never called and she didn't come back. For years I waited for her. I would always wonder why she left. This hole grew deeper and wider as the years passed. Her absence lefted me seeking other things and other people to fill the void and longing on the inside, but nothing worked.

Internally, I was haunted by voices that told me, "to just

let her go. she didn't want me, she will never come back for me, and that I meant nothing to her." The internal anguish tormented me because the love I had for my mom was unmatched, I loved her with all my being, but I couldn't get her out of my system.

Just when the memory of her began to dissipate, there she was, right back in my life along with my new baby sister. I was excited and angry at the same time. I was her baby girl and she left me, and now she had a new baby girl? A hard competition. How could I ever compete with this beautiful, adorable, baby? I had to get over it, but the feeling of not being wanted puzzled me and caused me to grow cold. Just when I started accepting my mother and baby sister's presence…just like a snap of the finger she was gone again with my baby sister with her. I was broken. For months I slept with my mother's robe and a small unused diaper from my baby sister's diaper bag. I kept each item as a keepsake. Every night I cried for them, but I knew for certain that this time she would not be coming back.

So, what does the spirit of rejection have to do with all of this? It has everything to do with this. This spirit was in full operation sinking its claws deep into my belief system before I could ever discover its attack. This kind of rejection beat me sore in my emotions and thoughts. For years, it left me feeling unwanted, and I still have remnants that I fight against this very day. This spirit had me selling myself short for many years. It's probably wreaked havoc in your life as well.

Listen, rejection will torment you. Like literally I was tormented. I so desperately wanted to be accepted that I would subject myself to environments that I know weren't good for me. I would stay in relationships that I knew were toxic. I would seek acceptance and attention in all the wrong ways. I wanted validation from others more than anything. I preferred attention and acceptance over genuine love. It didn't matter that the attention was empty and unauthentic. It didn't matter. I would accept any lie or false promises told to me because those empty words satisfied my need to belong. However, time has a way of partially numbing the pain.

As the years went by a little piece of the desire of having my mom around faded. When I think about it... I was never absent of the feeling of not being wanted, and I never stopped chasing after things that I thought could fill the void. One good thing I can say, is that in my search for acceptance. I never became promiscuous, but I did end up in dysfunctional relationships. The first person I lost my virginity to didn't even like me—he liked one of my cousins and they actually started to date shortly after. Then my first real boyfriend cheated on me repeatedly. It was awful, but I stayed because I wanted him to love me. I wanted him to accept me. I stayed with him for four years, and I convinced myself that one day we were going to get married and everything.

I just knew he was the one. He left our hometown and moved to Las Vegas to be with me. He had to love me right? Wrong, wrong, wrong! Within the first couple of months of him moving to Vegas, he cheated on me with a girl he barely knew and moved in with her. His same behavior followed us...

What was wrong with me? Why wasn't I enough? Why didn't he want me? Mesmerized by the feeling of just being wanted kept me putting up with his foolishness. Until one day I had enough. I was going to do to him what he had done to me. That's when I started to lose myself and begin to abandon my values. I coveted and sought out the attention of others just so I could make him jealous. He didn't care about the first time I went out and talked to someone else. The second time caught his attention, but he wasn't moved.

The third guy was my lowest, he had a child with another woman and told me that his son was a deceased nephew, and his son's mother was his deceased sister. I later found out the truth!

His double life caught up to him when I saw him with his family on my way to work one day. I couldn't take it anymore. I was right back at the beginning...right in the place where this was all too familiar...betrayal.

I was paralyzed and could feel that same pain clawing away at my heart. The same pain as from when my first boyfriend cheated. Eventually, I confront him and cut him loose. This pain caused me to be sucked right back into old patterns, and my drug of choice was my longtime boyfriend. Here I was again, intoxicated by his lies, and flattering lips. But, one day I woke up! I couldn't keep doing this! I had to stop! That day I made up in my mind that that this was going to be my last confrontation of his behavior. I demanded to know why he chose to use and abuse my heart, but even deeper I was wondering why that seemed to be the common theme in my life. I left him. I broke all ties to him, but by then I was a broken shell of a woman. "God, I just want you to send me somebody who would love me for me. Someone who real wants to love me." I prayed.

The spirit of rejection had free gain overtaking me with its power by setting up strongholds in my mind for years, but God intercepted and had my full attention. In 2002, I had an encounter with the kingdom of darkness that changed my life forever. After a night of smoking my problems away with laced marijuana. I began to hallucinate as me and my friend drove down Nellis Boulevard. I kept seeing this man standing in the street. From the passanger side, I grabbed at the wheel, causing us to sway through heavy traffic that could have caused a deadly accedient! But God! Once I made it back to my sisters apartment. I was extremely paranoid hearing voices and seeing demons. I was terrified. I put a blanket over my and and started praying. I cried out to the Lord and told Him that if He would took it away my pain and everything that I was experiencing that night I promised to serve Him with my life.

The very next day a friend of mine was knocking at my

door. She said that she kept hearing the Lord say Go get Patrea. So there she was. Standing at my doorstep. I could see that she was not going to leave without me. I search for an outfit that would be acceptable because it had been a minute since I had attended church. When I stepped into the sanctuary...I was overwhelmed with condemnation. The pastor spoke candidly and directly to me, and I knew it was God, because I didn't know this man, and it was like he was reading the chapters of my life, and even knew what I had done the night before attending service. I remember his words like it was yesterday. He said, "I hear the Lord saying, no matter what you did over the weekend, I still call and choose you." That was enough for me. I immediately bought a Bible, broke all ties with so-call friends, and committed to the process of changing my ways, rededicated my life to Christ, and that feeling of rejection...well, let's just say it took a break...for a while...

I was 18 years old when I seriously committed my life to Christ. I joined that church after attending a few times, and started working to change my ways. It was euphoric. I felt accepted, and I just knew they wanted me. Right? It's the church. Church people had to love broken and hurting people, right? Wishful thinking...church people are people trying to figure out their purpose too. Those who are in ministry are broken people too. Recovering people too. Sadly, not knowing this back then broke me even more. I was so mishandled in that ministry, and I wasn't the only one. I experienced more hurt from the people in church than I've yet to experience from the world, because I thought that these people should understand or should be loving me the way that they preached and sang about. I was angry and utterly disappointed, but I remained. I made a promise to God and I couldn't let Him down. Over time I see where I've made the same mistakes by unintentionally hurt others, because of my wounded soul just as some of those people made while in being in the church. Back then I had an all or nothing mentality. I now realize that getting hurt is inevitable. No matter what arena you find yourself in. What's the famous, but true phrase. "Hurting people, hurt people." However, I believe healed people can help heal people as well.

One thing about rejection is that it will rob us of time, growth, energy, lessons, and development. It keeps us so focused on what we are not and what we are not getting; life just flies right by us and its roots deepen. One day you'll look up and realize that you're still stuck in the same ol place. Tuh, listen. I was stuck.

I was angry and frustrated, I sat wondering how someone who was deemed joyful, special, funny, kind, loyal, warmhearted, and loving, could also be someone who felt so unwanted, neglected, and barely considered from those who said all of those wonderful things about me. It was puzzling to me. These thoughts made me angry. They made me bitter. How could people choose to love all the good things about me, but the moment I showed vulnerability, allowing them to see my weaknesses or my shortcomings—reduce me to nothing? So, much so that even when I was included, I still felt like I wasn't good enough to fit the mold of the group. Weird right? I had so many conflicting emotions as I was relying on others for completeness.

I found myself looking for something to fill all the voids. I tried to befriend person after person. I tried to act like other people. I tried buying things for other people, I tried paying off things for other people, I tried to do it like other people, but still, nothing worked. This emptiness I felt on inside haunted and taunted me. I couldn't escape the grip of its massive hands. With every squeeze, it seemed like life was being choked right out of me. Every attempt to fight back faded into the air like smoke; a diminished effortless attempt. I would pray, but it was like my prayers were hitting a glass ceiling. Every prayer bounced right back down on my head.

You see, back then I didn't know that rejection could attack in multiple ways. What I've learned over the years is that demonic spirits have a buddy system. Like in real life. These spirits partner together with other spirits to make our lives chaotic and purposeless. The moment I thought that I identified the cause of one thing, I found out that it seemed to be something else that would set me off. These spirits will have you doing things you thought you'd never do. They will cause you to normalize bad behavior, dismiss correction, discount accountability, and cause you to walk in pride. If we are not careful, these spirts will lure us in by entry of emotional wounds, disappointments, trauma, and other negative reactions such as anger, frustration, pride, and bitterness.

Listen...I was certain that I was perfectly fine. At some point, I was certain that I was loved. I was certain that I loved myself. But how could that be if I could come unraveled when I felt excluded or overlooked by anyone close to me? I was in a never-ending downward spiral and I couldn't seem to get my footing. I just wanted to stop feeling how I felt on the inside, and the more I desired to be accepted or acknowledged, the more I seemed deprived of the reassurance I sought after. The more I craved to be recognized, the more peace, joy, love, and acceptance I seemed to lose. I was being ROBBED by an invisible enemy.

Let me make this very clear, the spirit of rejection can show up in a variety of forms such as: being overlooked for a promotion, not getting the job you interviewed for, not being accepted into the college you desired, or not being accepted in the social circles or groups of people. The list goes on and on. Rejection along with fear, in my opinion, are the two powerful spirits that will attack anyone. No one is immuned or inescapable of its attacks. Especially, when we look to others as a source of approval and comfort.

Rejection, rebellion, and fear are found in every combination of the buddy system. If a person is battling the spirit of manipulation, at the core it's typically driven by rejection, rebellion, pride, and fear. This vicious cycle will go on and on with more spirits grouping together and building more strongholds.

Let's look at some definitions and meanings of rejection. By definition, rejection can refer to the act of rejecting something or the feeling one has after being rejected. In other words, you might have feelings of rejection after experiencing the rejection of others. The Biblical Counseling Database (BCD) breakdown of rejection states that the original meaning of the word rejection was *to throw back*.

The BCD states that "rejection occurs when a person or group of people excludes an individual and refuses to acknowledge or accept them." The KJV Dictionary definition of rejection is "to throw away, as anything useless or vile; to cast off; to forsake: to refuse to receive; to slight; to despise: to refuse to grant; as, to reject a prayer or request; to refuse to accept; as, to reject an offer."

No matter how it's worded or defined, rejection does not feel good. It is a destroyer of self-identity, self-confidence, self-worth, and self-value. It will destroy relationships and ultimately stagnate and foil the purpose in which God created you to fulfill. The evidence of rejection is found in those who have abandonment issues. Ding-ding-ding. I was one of those people. It attacks those who also struggle with an orphan spirit, who are fearful, and those who struggle with rebellion. The spirit of rejection is also tied to the life of a perfectionist and people-pleaser.

Please understand and be reminded that rejection is a demonic spirit. It's not just limited to an emotional feeling or belief. It's a demonic spirit that comes to oppress, depress, and drain you completely. It will make you forfeit every promise the Lord has spoken concerning you. It will keep you in perpetual cycles of defeat, second-guessing, confusion, complacency, comparison, and bondage.

As a matter of fact, rejection is the driving force causing victims to fall prey to its shouts, screams, and threats of not ever being good enough for anyone to accept them. But, can I proclaim this over your life? The devil is a liar! You will not for another second operate under the control of rejection! You will not accept the harassments of or stay in agreement with the spirit of rejection.

Today, I expose and disarm the power of every tactic, plot, poly, cohorts, and any other ensnarements connected to the spirit of rejection in the name of Jesus Christ. If we don't break the chains of rejection, it will keep us frozen in time. It will keep us stagnate, frustrated, fearful, and will arrest our development in the things that God has created us to produce. This spirit will rob you of your God-given identity. This spirit is not prejudiced. It does not care about how much money you have, how many people you know, how gifted you are, or how many degrees outlining your wall. Satan hates us!

Another thing about this spirit is that it is a spirit that can be classified as a "selfish" spirit because this spirit will cause its victims to be self-absorbed, self-seeking, and self-centered. *What about me? What are they going to say or think about me? No one wants to be around me. No one loves me.* You see...it will have you so stuck on you that you will be no use for others or to others.

If we're not careful, rejection will have us so infatuated by all of our weaknesses and inabilities; and how we're are not good at anything, or how much we're are not good enough. We won't even realize that over time we've disconnected ourselves from everything and everybody good for us. The agenda is to cripple and to destroy. To divide and conquer! Exposition is a must.

For years, this spirit has attacked me. I wrestled with deep-seated rejection that stemmed from the deep roots of multiple wounds. So please, understand that while I am writing about what I've experienced to encourage you that these feelings don't have to be a permanent fixture in your life; this is something I had to be delivered from. With the help of the Holy spirit, I had to expose it, I had confront it, fighting it, and refuse to accept it as my truth! I occasionally still have to remind the devil that I've been freed from this nasty spirit. Know and understand that even when we break free in an area as we receive our deliverance from any spirit, the enemy will come back to check our inventory to see if we have any open areas for him to occupy.

So, stay filled daily by the Spirit of God, by the Word of God, maitain consistent prayer, worship, personal intimate time with the Holy Spirit, and study of the Word. I know without a shadow of a doubt God has delivered me from the grips of this malicious spirit, and if God can do it for me, I am a 110% certain that he can do the same for you.

Deliverance from any demonic spirit is a process because we have to restructure our mindsets and belief systems that were damaged due to the oppression of demonic influence. That's not to say that God is unable to deliver you instantaneously, because I believe He absolutely can. I'm only speaking from my own experience, and I can only tell you that walking out your deliverance from rejection is a process, and you will and can be VICTORIOUSLY FREE from the bondage of rejection.

If you are truly ready to be released from the grips of rejection or any other demonic stronghold, you must be willing, to be honest, and expose it all. No shame, no guilt, and no embarrassment. Expose it all. To get a more in-depth look at the spirit of rejection, I highly recommend you snag this book by John Eckhardt, "*Destroying the Spirit of Rejection*".

Unmasking Fear

Like rejection, the spirit of fear is powerful. It too can be found in any cluster of demonic spirits. I'm almost certain that fear will be linked to every demonic spirit in which you seek deliverance from. What is fear? Some would break the word fear into the popular acronym *False Evidence Appearing Real*. I totally agree with that acronym as well. Webster's dictionary provides several different meanings of fear. I'm going to use what best fits everyone's understanding: to be afraid of: expect with alarm: FRIGHTEN; to be afraid or apprehensive.

I'm sure at one time or another we've come up against these feelings before. But why?

I believe that God placed an acute awareness in each of us to caution us of danger. During the time of man's fall, I believe that awareness was perverted from being something used to caution us to now causing us to be afraid. This was not God's original intent. God created each of us to rule with dominion and authority. Read Genesis Chapter 1.

When I reflect on my various stages of life (childhood, teenage, adult-hood), the spirit of fear was a prominent feature, and I didn't understand why. I was afraid of such mundane things. When I was little, I was scared of dogs and intimidated by people. I was creeped out by horror movies and scary stories. The ironic thing about that is even though I was terrified by horror movies and scary stories; I craved to watch them more, which only continued to feed the fear.

I know, I know...I bet you're like, "Patrea, it was just a movies though." Yeah, but what was behind the baseline of the movies? What was the producer's purpose in the movies? The purpose was to use imagery that would stimulate our natural senses using fear. If you're not raised in a household that provides proper covering through prayer and guarding the gates (eyes and ears) of your soul, then that door is left open for fear to come in and take residence.

Of course, there are other entry points where this spirit can enter in such as trauma. Fear can become deep-seated in a person who has experienced something traumatic which included: child abuse, molestation, domestic violence, witnessing of deaths, bullying, abandonment, or anything else similar and devastating.

Once the door is open to fear, just like wet metal, our souls begin to dull and become corroded. That fear starts to come alive. It begins to show up in our personalities, (she's just shy, oh she's just a little timid). Then it becomes normalized. It is alarming how the continuation and mounting of evidence of how fear is just categorized into thousand different types of phobias. We normalize fear and replace it with other names. Fear is fear. No matter what we name it! We have to expose it. Fear squats and hides in the background, and when it finally gets you alone it tries to paralyze you, intimidate, rule over you, and bully you. But that's only if you allow it to.

Think about it? If I were to ask you today why you felt stuck or stagnate in your purpose, what would be your reasoning as to why you have not yet stepped out to do what it is you feel you were called to do? What if I asked you to share something about yourself that you never shared before? What's the first feeling that would show up? Immediately, if those two questions were asked, we would find a list of fear-driven responses within.

*Fear of not being good enough

*Fear of inadequacy

*Fear of failure

*Fear of the opinions of others

*Fear of rejection

Fear prevents growth. The spirit of fear is a prison. I'm not telling you what I heard, I'm telling you what I know. If this spirit is not unmasked and disarmed, I promise you this spirit will show up in all areas of your life. Trust me, it might disguise itself as rejection, pride, or even being a strong woman or man; however, the root cause would still be FEAR. Fear, like all demonic spirits, will strip you of time and deprive you of life.

One thing I know about demonic spirits is that they cannot stay where they are not wanted. These spirits feed off the lies that you believe about yourself, about your current or past situation, and/or what you believe about others. Fear feeds off of our belief system. Oh, Jesus, let me say that again. The spirit of fear feeds off of our belief system. What we believe becomes our reality. Understand? What we believe becomes our reality. Fear causes our perception to be diluted, misconstrued, distorted, and disillusioned.

Whatever we believe becomes our truth, even if it's untrue. What a TRAP. Can I show you how fear is linked to other spirits? I won't go in-depth, but I want you to get an understanding of how vicious this spirit is.

rejection + fear = afraid that no one will accept or love you.

failure + fear = afraid of failing.

bitterness + fear = afraid to be vulnerable due to painful experiences causing an individual to self-protect using anger and resentment to mask fear.

Those are just a few examples, but if you examine your life closely and ask the Holy Spirit to shine the light on the area wherever fear has taken place in your life, you'll be surprised. However, we can rest in and on the truth of God's Word that declares to us:

"For God hath not given us the spirit of fear; but of power, and of love, and of a sound mind" (2 Timothy 1:7 KJV).[13]

"The Lord is my light and my salvation; whom shall I fear? The Lord is the strength of my life; of whom shall I be afraid? When the wicked, even mine enemies and my foes, came upon me to eat up my flesh, they stumbled and fell. Though a host should encamp against me, my heart shall not fear: though war should rise against me, in this will I be confident (Psalms 27:1-3 KJV)[14].

The only way to break the grips of fear is the truth of God's word. It may not happen right away. Remember, these spirits have been setting up residence in our souls for years, so daily we must transform and renew our minds with the Word of God and renounce everything attach to fear until everything is uprooted.

"And do not be conformed to this world, but be transformed by the renewing of your mind, that you may prove what is that good and acceptable and perfect will of God." Romans 12:2 (NKJV)[15]

Plus, we have nothing to fear. The Lord is our light, and He is our salvation. Jesus came to save that which was lost. He came to set the captive free. Refuse to fear. Take back your authority. Take back your voice. Don't allow fear to rule over you. Expose it all.

On a sheet of paper, I would like for you to take this moment to renounce and denounce fear. After you finish crumble that paper up and throw it in the trash where it belongs!

Renounce-formally declares one's abandonment of; reject and stop using or consuming.

Denounce- publicly declare to be wrong or evil.

EX. I RENOUNCE AND DENOUNCE THE FEAR OF FAILURE, AND

ANY SPIRITS TIED TO FEAR. IN JESUS NAME. *(You can also follow up with the scriptures referenced in this chapter to support your stance).* AND I REPLACE IT WITH THE TRUTH OF GOD'S WORD. THAT I HAVE NOT BEEN GIVEN THE SPIRIT OF FEAR, BUT OF POWER, LOVE, AND A SOUND MIND.

Search the scripture. Google scriptures in the areas you struggle with. There are so many free resources out there that you can use.

Unmasking Anger/Rage

The year of 2015 was a heart wrenching, heartbreaking, and a heart checking kinda' season for me. I believe this year was the straw that broke the camel's back. I struggled emotionally and psychologically. I was on ten, like always. The pain of betrayal, constant feelings of being rejected, and not being heard vexed me. Even though I willed myself to be as consistent as I could be, it was slowly chipping away at me. I would maintain consistency by being present and showing up for others, but I was feeling so neglected, pushed aside, and used that I was diminishing. Joy evaded me. I wasn't getting what I needed from the people I thought I should be getting the support from. I felt like my needs were pushed aside and ignored.

You see, I've always prided myself on being a loyal, faithful, giving, and kind-hearted person and friend; but during this time of my life everything around me was going dark. I started to hate those qualities about myself because I felt like everyone around was benefitting from my good qualities except for me. I was giving and supporting, but I felt like my needs or how I felt didn't matter. I continued to serve at my local church, encouraged and challenged those who I was connected to, but I felt empty. I began to resent a lot of things and people. I became a ticking time bomb waiting to explode at any given moment.

I started to react to certain situations that under normal circumstances wouldn't warrant a reaction. I was becoming unglued, but I didn't want to disappoint anyone. After a while, I started becoming angry with myself for not speaking up for me. It wasn't okay for others to unload their thoughts and feeling regarding me in my not so great moments, and not allow me to unload my feelings regarding how they responded towards—or how they spoke to— or how they treated me when having their bad moments. I just sat there and took it, because I wanted to be loved and accepted by them. I found myself in that same cycle I once had in previous relationships.

This made me mad and shameful. Why was I even allowing it this to happen again? I didn't recognize how bad it was until I started to have this inconsolable anger, disappointment, and GRIEF on the inside. I began to punish myself for feeling this way. I began to self-reject which led to more anger and more, and more; until I was ENRAGED.

What was happening to me? I started to compare myself to the people around me and started sizing myself up to how other people treated them; versus how they treated me. I began to feel like I was standing in the shadows of others. It was like I was back at square one. I didn't get it.

"BACK TO SQUARE ONE"

It was like I was eighteen year old girl all over again, who had joined a ministry thinking that everthing would be different. I didn't know that ministry would cause so much damage! The leadershp broke me, and changed the trajectory of my life.

During that time, I was just getting in the swing of church ministry things. I knew about Jesus and salvation and all, but now I was serious about my salvation, but of course, I was not fully delivered. I was only 18. I still had worldly cravings and appetites that I had not yet overcome, but I was definitely putting up a good fight and putting my best foot forward. I made several mistakes along the way but was determined to live for God. As time passed, I wanted to commit even more.

This led to "The Anderson Season" of my life. What was "The Anderson Season"? Well, it was when I naively begged and convinced my husband to move from Las Vegas to Atlanta for what I thought to be fulfilling the purpose of God. I pleaded and pleaded. I wanted to please God and I wanted to do everything in His will, so I left my extended family to serve, follow, and build another man's vision that I thought God was calling me to do. I had no clue what would come...

The idea that we were moving to do kingdom work by ministering the gospel of Jesus and starting a new church was short-lived. I found myself in the center of absolute horror, derailment, utter shock, mental distress, emotional turmoil, and abuse by the only pastor I personally knew..."Pastor Anderson" I had so much respect for this person. I truly admired, regarded, and respected this person as my spiritual leader, and I was devastatingly heartbroken and hurt.

This person broke my spirit, caused me to abandon the feelings of trust for people that I once had; and sadly, caused my family and me great emotional damage. Here was another time where I just took the blows by not standing up for myself or communicating my thoughts out of fear of not being wanted. Do you see how the spirit of rejection and anger partnered together to gain leverage over my soul? This is why it's important to stay connected to God, and not set your worship on the person. Anyhow...

I concluded that I would not let this person win. My resolve was to suppress my feelings, ignore everything, and just leave. My husband and I left, and we never addressed any issues or feelings we had—we just left carrying the wounds, frustration, and irritations.

However, not dealing with everything was not a good idea at all, because "what goes in must come out".
We left Anderson's home, and my family and I started to revamp and reconnect to life once again. This transition was difficult for all of my family. We had to work hard to readjust to just being the four of us without the extra drama.

My little family of four felt the effects of this gut-wrenching, heart-twisting, and soul fragmenting recovery process. Whew. The process of recovery was grueling. Some of the effects were almost undetected for some time. I didn't know seeds of destruction were concealed and sealed with a warm smile just waiting to germinate, bud, and grow. Life went on and we learned to live around the giant elephant in our room. We overlooked the night terrors; we overlooked the emotional instability in us and our children.

We overlooked the damage that had taken place in our thoughts, lives, emotions, and spirituality. We were oblivious to what was taking place on the inside of us. We were just happy and satisfied that we finally had some sense of peace. We were able to sleep, and we felt our atmosphere was calm. We were grateful that we made it out of the situation alive. Unknowingly the internal damage was already done.

You see, we never took into consideration how dangerously fragmented we were. Every area of our lives were affected by the "Anderson Season" we experienced. We blissfully ignored what we went through and swept it right under the rug. My husband and I did not realize our marriage was in jeopardy or that one of our son had adopted anger issues from this season. We didn't really want to face the fact that we both were in an abusive cult-like situation.

So, can you imagine what was lurking at the core of our being at this point? The spirit of rejection was still being fed there. Fear was still living there. Now, this vicious spirit gained some counterparts.

Months went by and my husband and I began to sober up a bit, and we started to attend church again. We started to talk to new people. Of course, we played it safe and were careful not to rush into anything, but, the way my personality is set up, and the love I have for people left me conflicted and overly cautious. I love people genuinely, but I was wounded.

I was no longer the lively Patrea that left Las Vegas for Georgia. This Patrea moved differently, she thought differently, and even though she had a host of issues before, she was now weighted with insurmountable bondage. Isolation was the drug of choice. It was my numbing antidote. It kept me safe. At least that's what I thought.

Like I've mentioned before, I love people but keeping them at a distance was the goal back then. I made inner vows to never let anyone get as close as I did with the Andersons ever again. I loved people, but I no longer believed that people truly could or would love me as I loved them.

Do you see the pattern? Rejection, Anger, and Fear. The same message suggested to me when I was a young girl. I've now come into agreement with it. "No one would love me or want me."

Months had passed by, and my husband and I start mingling and mixing; we were living again...guarded but none the less living. Different things began to happen, and I continued to isolate and suppress my feelings and thoughts. And, if you've never dealt with isolation and suppression of emotions, just know that it's a deadly mix. Years had gone by, and I started to come out of my shell. I made a few friends and allowed myself to be a bit vulnerable.

However, Anderson continued to make his threats, and

his presence known. It was horrible. Eventually, we had to get a restraining order. Anderson really did a number on us, and some of the others who packed up their lives to follow him to serve others did too. We were all vulnerable and victims. Unfortunately, Anderson continued with this repeated destructive pattern of behavior which led him to commit a murder-suicide in 2017 on my birthday.

After the experience from being under his leadership; for years I carried disdain for people who were in a place of leadership that would intentionally hurt and manipulated people for their own personal gain. I ended up lacking grace and empathy for those who were just being human, and having hard moments.

So, the moment I felt that feeling from anyone I would shut down immediately; not knowing that power still ruled over my emotions, and my beliefs. I had to get this thing off of me. I had to tell what happened to us during all those years under his leadership.

So, I began to share little by little with caution about some of the things we endured while living with Anderson. I desired to trust again, so I started to step out of my safety net a little, but at the same time felt like I was somehow I was being disloyal to this man who threatened our lives.

I continued pressing through this newfound pasture of life, and it seemed like smooth sailing, but it was not. There were days where I felt like I was becoming too connected and close to others, so, you guessed it; I began to self-destruct to self-protect. It was as if I went into a survival mode. I was not going to be bamboozled again. I was not going to be lied to and hurt again. Some days I would be open and pleasant and other days I would be distant and disconnected. And, not just with those around me, I was even this way towards my husband. We both picked up coping mechanisms.

It angered me. I was constantly angry and on edge. This was not me. Where was all of this coming from? I was certain that I was over this stuff. What was going on with me? Little by little I felt like "Patrea" was drifting away, but I kept pushing. Saying to myself, *"You've got this Patrea, just keep going."* I've always been a fighter even if it would cause my detriment, I would push through it. I refused to break or give in. I refused to let whatever this was have power over me. I kept right on pushing even though it became toxic, which is exactly what happened in 2015. So, let us go back there...

Even though the "Anderson Season" of my life was up, the damage was already done. I found myself destitute of identity and self-worth. The continual comparison of myself to others caused jealousy to grow. I became self-destructive and started to abusively criticize myself inwardly and outwardly. I couldn't remember being envious of others before...well not at this level. Of course, I was a bit insecure from time-to-time, but not to the point of wanting to be someone else.

My inner conversations grew dark and were deadly. The outcry of the pain inside reflected in my behavior. However, those around me didn't know what was going on inside of me, and so, my actions were judged harshly. I was under attack and sinking quickly. I was sinking and no one seemed to care, and if they did care, then they just had to inform me each time of how they had come to my rescue time and time again. But when I did the same back, it was a problem. I thought to myself...

I thought love kept no record. Just quoting that piece of scripture would set me off. Oh, the colloquialisms. I began to hate people. I was furious! I thought of all the times I showed up during others' times of need and had allowed them to be themselves. Yet, here I was sinking. I wondered where they were now that I needed them. I didn't know how to stop it, nor did I know how to properly articulate it. All I did know was, I didn't want to be this way, but there I was…ANGRY. Angry about it all.

I found that when I tried to express my feelings, share my thoughts, or give my perspective on how I felt I was being treated; the tables would turn; only to leave me feeling even more unheard, neglected, disregarded, and frustrated. It appeared as though everyone else was concerned about how the other person or persons were feeling more than what I felt or was feeling. Or even what I was saying. What I was going through was about me, but it felt like it was always about them. I felt that other peoples' feelings took precedent over my own. I felt like they were more important. So, what was the point?

Once again, I found myself stuffing back my feelings, thoughts, and concerns. I didn't want those relationships to end, so I would bottled up my concerns. Even during times when I could share my concerns, I no longer desired to express myself. I would just apologize and go on. I felt like my feelings no longer mattered, so there was no need to open up. It seemed pointless.

I started to close up more and more. What others said no longer mattered. I went back into the archive of my soul and was comforted by my former thoughts. *Don't trust anyone.* I even acquired some new ones, *don't fall in love with their words, look at their actions instead. Words of people are only words for the moment. Their words won't hold water. You got the proof of this.*

I was struggling. I stayed defensive and protective of my needs. I began to tell myself that I was all alone and that I only had to fight for myself and my family because no one else ever would. I told myself that no one cared about me or us. A lot a self-loathing, right? But at the time those were my true, real, uncensored feelings and interpretations. Now, I'm not saying those feelings were correct.

However, they were my reality for a long while. I learned very quickly that if you don't communicate what you need, people with give what they think you need, and it will still be ineffective. I needed something but couldn't articulate what I needed. At some point, I learned how to communicate what I needed, but I refused to be let down again, and I didn't want to express what was triggering my pain. Plus, my trust was severed.

This spirit of anger had a hold of me. It had me so focused on the offenses of others, and my shortcomings I couldn't see God's love, grace, or mercy in anything. Everything started to unravel. My relationships were dissolving, and I had no more fight to give. I was just simply waiting for them to all end. I went from loving and caring for people to absolutely hating people. My heart was inconsolable, and I was checked out. My body would show up to church gatherings and events, but my heart was no longer in it. Then transition happened within the church. You know it's bad when you get demoted within the church. I'd reached rock bottom.

Ironically, even though all the pain, disappointment, shame, regrets, and heartache I endured; my heart still surprisingly remained tender towards God. Of course, I didn't want to feel this way, but I told God at the age of 18 that if he would save me from that one situation...I would serve Him for the rest of my life. I was angry, but I was willing to work through it. Now, that I shared the turn of multiple events in my life and emotions, can you see how rejection can link up with spirits?

The spirit of anger/rage will drive you emotionally crazy and cause you to do crazy and reckless things. Trust me on this. The definition of anger is a strong feeling of annoyance, displeasure, or hostility. According to bibletools.com, anger is defined as a "strong emotional reaction of displeasure, often leading to plans for revenge or punishment." Once this spirit is in operation, you will have to expose its tentacles immediately. This spirit will have you plotting and planning the demise of others, but you'll be the one falling faster and hitting the ground quicker.

Anger opens the doors to other spirits such as bitterness, unforgiveness, and hatred to name a few. This spirit will cause you to be impulsive and paranoid. This spirit will cause you to be isolated and lonely because people will start removing themselves from your presence. Another thing that I've learned about this spirit is that it doesn't necessarily have to be loud and obnoxious. It moves in quietly; it's very subtle and passive, yet it is powerfully present.

If overpowered and unrestrained, anger will morph into wrath, and it will consume you. I know a few people right now who have chosen to hang on to anger for so long that years have passed them by, and rage and wrath have consumed them. Everyone around them deals with it, and even those around them have now embraced that same spirit and they don't even realize they are operatating under the same influence. The spirit of anger can and will blind you.

Sadly, time will pass you by, and years will be wasted, and those who you are/were angry with have moved on with life, and you will be stuck in the same place with the same anger feeding off the original pain and offense. The spirit of anger will steal your joy and bankrupt you of peace. Expose it and unmask this spirit. Leave no room and leave no gaps or openings. Even Jesus warns that angry people will face God's judgment. See Matthew 5:22. Scripture also tells us to be quick to listen, slow to speak, and slow to be angry. See Proverbs 16:32

I could have stayed in that place. I could have held on to that anger, but if I did, it wouldn't have changed anything. I had a right to be angry, but it wasn't worthy of the place where God was taking me. I had the right to be angry about everything that transpired throughout the years of my life, but it still wasn't worth my freedom. You may share these same sentiments but trust me on this... it's not worthy of the place where God wants to take you, and it's not worth your freedom either.

I now have this understanding that I'm not deprived of choice. I have the choice to choose to be free and so do you. Expose it ALL. Don't let Satan typecast you into misery. His job is to steal, kill, and destroy you.

Unmasking Pride

Another despicable spirit is the spirit of pride. This demonic spirit is dangerous because it's subtle and can veil itself and cause the individual to believe that they are behaving honorably somehow. This spirit will cause a person to forfeit their freedom with soft and smooth suggestions.

You know what I'm talking about…we say with our mouths, "oh I'm fine I don't need any help," but really and truly we do. Or how about, "I'm going to show them that I don't need them." Yep, it's all pride. Pride can mask itself in false humility and arrogance. And…yes, there is a healthy pride. For instance, those parents who pride in their children on their accomplishments, growth and development, and of their other milestones. This, not the kind of pride I'm referencing. I'm speaking about the spirit of pride that suffocates the joy out of life.

I've literally been ensnared by the spirit of pride too. I know individuals who refuse to let go of pride. They literally deprived themselves and others of meaningful relationships and the opportunity to heal, grow, learn, mature, and live a life that is enriching. Sadly, they've spent years in torment, because they are too prideful to apologize for their poor behavior, poor decisions, and refusal to unforgive. Time has passed them by, and they are still rehearsing and rehashing mixtures of lies and truth—which breed confession. Pride says, "I'm right and when wrong."

So, yes. It can come in a form of refusing to admit faults. This is not to say that sometimes you may be right about how you are feeling or right concerning a situation, but if you know you are wrong about an action, or if you know you made the wrong decision but refuse to admit it because you think the other person(s) will win? It's PRIDE... Anytime you have the opportunity to humble yourself and expose yourself and choose not to, it's not only pride it is sin. *"Therefore, to him who knows to do good and does not do it, to him it is sin"* James 4:17 (NKJV)[16].

The spirit of pride always masque itself as strength, you know what I mean? You may need some groceries or may need some gas money to get to work, but you don't want to expose the fact that you are having a hardship, so you suffer instead. Nope. That is not strength. It's PRIDE. If you know you can receive help without judgment but refuse, then that is PRIDE.

Pride also can be described as having an exceedingly high self-regard.[17] In other words, IT'S ALL ABOUT ME, IT'S ALL ABOUT HOW I FEEL, AND I DON'T CARE WHO GET'S HURT IN THE CROSSFIRE. NO EXCEPTIONS.

Other definitions of pride reference it as a FOOLISHLY, IRRATIONAL CORRUPT SENSE OF ONE'S PERSONAL VALUE, STATUS, OR ACOMMPLISHMENT.[18] Whew, Jesus help us TODAY. Did you read that? Read it out loud one more time. It says pride in essence will have us looking foolish, cause us to be irrational, and our character (what we're made of and what we value most, our morals) will be corrupt. Pride will have us behaving from a crooked place of thinking, feeling, and how we conduct ourselves. So much so that our perception is skewed. The way we process things will be off. Our realities twisted, and the lines of truth blurred. Oh my gosh. I know this to be TRUE. I'm not telling you what I heard. I'm telling you what I know!

Pride breaks up marriages. Pride hinders growth. Pride keeps us hurting. Pride robs us of love. Pride keeps us bound to the offense. Pride deprives us of assistance/help. Pride is a false sense of balance... A false sense of balance is an abomination to God. Check out the scripture. "A false balance is abomination to the LORD: but a just weight is his delight" Proverbs 11:1 (KJV)[19]. Pride says, "*I have everything under control, and everything is balanced*." But in reality, everything is off-balance, and full of chaos. It's a lie.

We've all been here before. No shame. We have. Just the place where the devil wants us to die. Right, in the pit of destruction—clothed in false honor.

We can also find the spirit of pride lurking around those who have experienced some form of devastation, anguish, pain, or trauma at some point in time in their life. So, that individual ends up robed in pride to deflect from the pain that they are going through. Pride will have this person going to extreme measures to justify their actions no matter if they are right or wrong. I am just scratching the top of the surface with this spirit. The roots of this spirit grow deep. What I can tell you is that this spirit is linked to fear, offense, rejection, and bitterness. This is what God's Word says about pride: *"Pride goeth before destruction, and a haughty spirit before a fall"* (Proverbs 16:18 (KJV)[20].

Pride is also on the list of things God hates. Let us look at that list Proverbs 6:16-19 (NKJV)[21] *"These six things the Lord hates, Yes, seven are an abomination to Him: A proud (prideful) look, A lying tongue, hands that shed innocent blood, A heart that devises wicked plans, Feet that are swift in running to evil, A false witness who speaks lies, And one who sows discord among brethren."*

Pride displeases God. It will cause destruction and cause us to fall at the risk of trying to be right. Pride is like a hospital gown. Everything is covered up together in the front, but when you turn around and your backside is all out! Pride is a despicable spirit, and it MUST BE EXPOSED AT ALL COST.

At this point, I hope you can see some similarities and can relate to some of the feelings I had and shared. Even if you have not had the exact same experiences. Let me say this...

there's nothing wrong with you. It's just that you have some issues of the soul accompanied by some unwanted/unwelcome guest that need to be dispelled. Let's continue to expose and unmask these enemies and cohorts who are in pursuit to arrest our development and vex our souls.

Unmasking Orphan Spirit

Have you ever had a time where you just wished you could just be—be your own authentic self? No masks, no worries, no comparisons, and no cowering behind the opinions of others? To be that person who is free to make mistakes, free to learn from failures, and free to cry at times because sometimes you feel life sucks—and people still love and adore you? Well, let me tell you, I have been in the same position, and felt this way before. I was made aware of the spirit of orphan after purchasing the book, *The Esther's Anointing,* by Michelle McClain-Walters.

I learned that an orphan spirit will cause a person to operate and function from a place of performance to gain approval or acceptance from people. It's a people-pleasing spirit. As you saw between the pages of this here book—it was definitely evident that I was also bound by this spirit as well. This is why we must know at the core of our being our true identity and understand our value and worth to God first. We have to learn how to develop this self-love and fall in love with who God credits us to be. If not, we'll find ourselves trying to earn love and acceptance by the things we can do, buy, or give. An orphan spirit drives us to perform, and when our performance falls short, unfortunately, we are left with the broken pieces.

This is all too familiar. After transitioning from the role administrator of my church, I felt empty. "If I'm not doing anything here in the church who's going to love me?" I thought to myself. Right then God started the stripping process. Everything I did for Him (God) and for people was from the perspective if I could just do...He will love me—they will love me. If I couldn't work or do it right, then I felt like couldn't or wouldn't receive the love from the person I sought love from. Twisted, right?

As far as I can go back, I remember this feeling. I worked all my life from this place. In school with my friends and teachers, in my relationships, in my family, and in ministry. Always working to be loved. Always working to be accepted. But, what happens when we're traded in for something new. What if what we could no longer produce what the other person needs?

What would happen? If we only work for love and acceptance; we put a limit on yourself. Plus, you've now allowed those people to determine your worth. That's exactly what happened to me. I could no longer produce, and the other people went on with life and never looked back. I was the only one left picking up the pieces, even though I put my all into everything I did. It was a hard pill to swallow, but I had to take responsibility for it all. I allowed that kind of treatment and I didn't set boundaries. I was so desperate for love that I diminished what I was carrying by performance.

This spirit will cause you to work aimlessly after the heart of people who may or may not even care. You may or may not get a "job well done". This spirit causes you to look for the applause from people instead of being captivated by God's heart, and unfailing love and acceptance of you.

I was traded out quickly and became an afterthought. This wounded my soul and broke my heart. I thought at least I mattered a little bit. After all, I gave and all I did? I would have thought...I mattered...or what I did count for something, but in an instant "POOF" that was it. This showed me a lot about love, my own heart, and the hearts and motives of others. Today, I have no expectations...no hidden expectation either. I do things of my own accord and expect nothing in return. I have also learned how to categorize people accordingly because their actions revealed to me their true character. For instance, some relationships ended after I stopped performing, some relationships consist of individuals calling when they were in need, and then there were those who only called to probe to see if I had the latest cup of tea (gossip)—I was definitely not the one for that! And, then there was of course the ones who were truly genuine and our relationship was a reciprocal gift of friendship and love.

It's still a battle for me because sometimes there are days that I truly feel lonely but in those moments... I learned the phrase, "DON'T DO IT PATREA". I had to fight against the urge to do something for some just to receive their company. (Don't fall for the trap)! There were times when I caved and would go out of my way to do things for others just to receive words of affirmation from them. Now that I think about it all. I can own it, but back then it hurt me greatly because the recipient didn't understand the place of pain that sourced my generosity. So please beware of the schemes and tricks of this spirit. Love is not earned, instead, it is given freely. I don't want to say love doesn't cost, because Jesus paid a hefty price that expressed His love for us all. But when I look back at His act of love... it didn't cost Him anything...He was willing to give His life for us. Man, I'm so glad I'm loved by Him. Okay, okay...

Some time ago, I came across a 2013 article from Charisma Magazine titled, "The Difference between the Orphan Spirit and a Spirit of Sonship". In this article, the author uncovers some really interesting traits about the orphan spirit. I also identified another trait that I feel is closely related to the orphan spirit and that is "perfectionism". Not only did I perform for love... whatever I did had to be perfect, and if it was not, I would judge and penalize myself harshly. I would put undue stress and pressure on myself, and for years I tried to be this "Perfect Being". I tried to be this perfect wife, perfect mother, perfect daughter/sibling, perfect employee, perfect person in ministry, perfect in relationships, and just overall perfect. I'm far from it. Today, I just try to work to be "BETTER" not perfect.

I've wasted years beating myself up, because I disappointed people I loved or if I couldn't help others (financially, emotionally, or for anything—you name it…). Slowly but surely everything around me began to come apart. Can you say "DISASTER"? Yep, a hot-flaming mess. I was a walking disaster. My imperfections made me look at things differently. I became unhappy, unpleasant, and honestly a waste. I was striving to be everything people wanted me to be or trying to prove to people that I was the opposite of what they may have believed about me. Especially if it wasn't true. At this point everything became exhausting…just merely existing was a drag.

I finally had to come to the point where the rubber met the road, and I had to tell myself, that I wasn't perfect and that it was perfectly normal to make mistakes as long as I could learn from them as I kept growing. As a matter of fact, I had to learn that I was created to be ME. Me with all my imperfections and idiosyncrasies. So often we take what I call "Growing Experiences" (mistakes/failures) and try our best to avoid them, and in doing so we make bigger messes because we feel like we have to cover for the mistakes and failures or allow the mistakes or failures to define us causing us to go into a performance frenzy. Instead, we should take the opportunities to learn and grow from them.

You see, we are slaves if there is anything controlling and dominating us by keeping us confined. The orphan spirit will initiate a transference of perfectionism onto whatever we are trying to portray. It is the pretense of making everything look like we have it all together and under control, but in reality— the truth of the matter is— well, we are coming apart, right at the seams.

God's honest truth is that we need help and an outlet to grow, mature, and develop properly in those underdeveloped areas of our lives. Without performance and without perfection, but a place of genuine love, understanding, empathy, and trust; that cultivate a safe place for true humility and a sincere surrender.

Again, deliverance is work. Just because you pray six times, dance and shout four times, and sing worship songs all week—you will not instantly receive your break-through. The bible puts it this way, "Therefore, my beloved, as you have always obeyed, not as in my presence only, but now much more in my absence, work out your own salvation with fear and trembling." [22]

The Word also tells us that action needs to be taken in order for some things to depart from us, "However, this kind does not go out except by prayer and fasting."[23] It's work. It requires sacrifice and willingness to be free. Deliverance from these spirits just don't fall from the sky. You have to be determined to eradicate them from your life indefinitely.

I had to come to a place where I said, "God...I need You. Please come in and be the perfecter of my life. You are able, You are capable, You are faithful, and Lord You are willing to do what You promised concerning in my life." I had to lay down my "perfection" and I had to embrace all of my imperfections because those imperfections made me relatable. Those imperfections taught me to be teachable. Those imperfects made up all of who I thought I would never be. My decision set something in motion and began to produce the woman I'm becoming.

I am who I am, and who I'm predestined to be because God refused to give up on me. Guess what. I didn't have to perform for His grace and mercy either. That's what He gave me willingly. He will do the same for you too. Let me say this. Never discount your trip-ups and down-falls. God uses everything.

Yes, everything. I'm just crazy enough to believe that He will use the very thing that was meant to destroy us to become the launching pad to catapult us into our purpose. God didn't create us to be perfect, because He foreknew our imperfection "the sin of man" would cause us to stumble, but He can and He does perfect those things that concern us. Hallelujah! Now that's something to get excited about!

Let's take a minute to unmask the orphan spirit. After being enslaved by this spirit and freed from this spirit I've gained so much insight about how this spirit operates and preys. First, let's look at the meaning of the word orphan. It is described as being a person whose parents have died, are unknown, or have permanently abandoned them. In order to fully understand this spirit, I want to reference the aforementioned article from Charisma Magazine. I noted some of the traits that I could relate to, and that I personally experienced. Perhaps you can relate to some of these traits I found in the article as well.

The orphan spirit operates out of insecurity and jealousy.
Those oppressed by an orphan spirit will constantly battle jealousy and insecurity. Since the original source of security is found in the relationship we have with our parents, those oppressed by an orphan spirit are insecure, and they have a hard time hearing a biological or spiritual father or mother praise their siblings or co-laborers.

The orphan spirit is jealous of the success of others.
Those oppressed by this spirit are happy when others are failing because it makes them feel good about themselves.

The orphan spirit lacks self-esteem.
Those oppressed by the orphan spirit have difficulty loving and accepting themselves. These individuals self-reject, self-hate, and self-destruct.

The orphan spirit serves God and others to earn love.
We've talked about this. Those oppressed by this spirit is con-

stantly striving to earn the Father's love and the love of other people through their accomplishments in ministry, careers, or in their deeds.

The orphan spirit uses people as objects to fulfill goals.
Those oppressed by an orphan spirit tend to use people as objects to accomplish their goals. Those with this spirit will reduce the value of people for the fulfillment of their objectives. They manipulate with words, threats, and anything necessary to have their way to control.

The orphan spirit experiences anger and fits of rage.
Those oppressed by an orphan spirit have issues with self-control and anger. They have bouts of rage and use different types of manipulation tactics because they feel inferior, so they must control others to fill their insecurity while pushing their personal agendas. Why? Because they lack trust in the plan that God has for their future.

The orphan spirit is always in constant competition with others.
Those oppressed by the orphan spirit will always, and I mean *always* try to outshine others. No matter the time, place, or opportunity because of how they perform is their identity.

Now, this last trait is a DOOZIE.

The orphan spirit receives its primary identity through material possessions, physical appearance, and activities.

Those oppressed by the orphan spirit will never be satisfied with career success, educational success, material possessions, pleasure, or illicit relationships. Because of toxicity within, there will never be enough to fill the void in their identity. Consequently, they are mostly satisfied by things, people, and their appearance; such as clothes, excessive amounts of tattoos, skin piercings, and hairstyles—can be their way of standing out as unique as a cry for attention due to a lack of self-esteem and fatherly affirmation.

Whew, now let that marinate. This is why it's important to self-evaluate and ask God to reveal what's within us. The devil does not want you to fulfill your God-given purpose. He wants you to DIE. He wants you to believe you are not loved, accepted, wanted, or cared for! He perverts everything and lies continually! The devil can't tell the truth if he wanted to! Now you see why it important that you need to unmask and expose this gross spirit?. Those who fall prey to this spirit are broken, insecure, and lack the ability to receive and embrace true love in its purest form because they feel that they have to perform for it in order to get it, but the only way to break freedom is to unmask and disarm it. Reflect on this.

Take a real close look at yourself...do any of these traits depict your behavior? Here is the moment of truth. If you can identify with one or more, then you are in the right place for deliverance. Deliverance can only happen when you are open and honest about where you are. In addition, you must desire to be totally free from oppression and bondage from these demonic spirits holding you captive.

Lastly, I feel like unmasking the spirit of offense. This spirit will destroy our connectivity to individuals assigned to our purpose! The effects of this spirit can be felt and so many can relate to the impact that this spirit has on the life of anyone who encounters it. In order to minister effectively, be used by God at any capacity, or even be a person of godly influence—we must be delivered from the spirit of offense.

Unmasking Offense

Some years back I went into a Christian Book Store, and I know for sure that the Holy Spirit led me to this book titled *The Bait of Satan*, by John Bevere. This is another book you can add to your library. It's a must-read if you constantly battle the spirit of offense.

This is what John says about those who have the spirit of offense:

> Offended people produce much fruit, such as hurt, anger, outrage, jealousy, resentment, strife, bitterness, hatred, and envy. Some of the consequences of picking up an offense are insults, attacks, wounding, division, separation, broken relationships, betrayal, and backsliding. Often those who are offended do not even realize they are trapped. They are oblivious to their condition because they are so focused on the wrong that was done to them. They are in denial. The most effective way for the enemy to blind us is to cause us to focus on ourselves.][24]

I am in total agreement with him. Offense, along with fear and rejection, is very self-centered. The focus is always on SELF. A person under attack by this spirit can never see where they erred. Like its partner "Pride" this demonic spirit will have you so focused on pain or the offense, that sadly, that the person doesn't even realize that they've been ensnared. As a matter of fact, they feel as though they have a right to feel how they feel. Maybe so, but we have to understand that our feelings cannot be trusted! Even if we are right, we still must develop a way of letting unhealthy reactions go.

The spirit of offense slowly and methodically sucking the life out of its victim. It destroys their discernment and causes them to be out of touch with their behavior and the reality of the behavior of others. They can't see their wrongs—only the wrong of others—never seeing the disconnect. Slowly, but surely their relationship buckle, and they can't comprehend why people no longer want them to be in their presence. They wonder why no one wants to answer their phone calls, and they do not understand why family and friends don't want to invite them to the outings. Ha! I was in that boat. I've been delivered for some time, and some people still do not want me around. However, I'm fine with that. I understand that damage may cause great strain. I also learned that everyone is not going to embrace your growth...and that's on them not you.

Those who battle offense fail to comprehend that this spirit is like a dark cloud that hovers everywhere they go. They are so well acquainted with it that they want others to carve out space for their bad habits deriving from this spirit. No. This is unacceptable. No. Your offense should not be welcomed. If this is you, then it's time to let go! It's time to let go of being offended by things that happened to you over sixteen, seventeen, twenty, or forty years ago.

If people sincerely apologized for their offense towards you, be willing to forgive them and move on. Forgiveness is for you not for the one who hurt you. Yes, I'm fussing about this, because an unforgiving heart opens the door for the tormentor. I don't want you to waste years of your life. I don't want you to remain stuck in pain and in a place that no longer serves your purpose. Trust me...I've wasted so much time, energy, and tears — and those things will never change what happened to me.

However, we've been given the ability to produce something new through the power of CHOICE, and through the power of FORGIVENESS. Now, this is not to negate what or has happened to you. This is not to excuse what was done to you, but this is me presenting to you an opportunity to give you back your POWER and your AUTHORITY. This is me giving you the opportunity to LIVE again, HOPE again, TRUST again, and DREAM again. Don't let offense demobilize you or stunt your development. Can I pose these questions to you? I really want you to think about them too.

Does being offended change the way you feel about the situation? Has being offended helped you grow in a positive way? Has being offended allowed you to see life in a positive light? How has being offended served you? How much time have you wasted being offended? How many of your relationships have been broken by being offended?

Did you really ponder those questions? Were you really honest with yourself?

When dealing with an offense, you have to only deal with you. You own your stuff only. That's what strips the enemy of his power. You choose to let it go of your right completely. Now, I would be lying to you if I were to say doing this is a breeze through the park. No, it's not going to always be easy, but it necessary. You are worth fighting for, so don't tap out of the fight! Go harder and come out on the other side with victory!

One more thing I want to share with you. The spirit of offense can also cause sickness in the body. So, if you are struggling in your body, you might want to evaluate what you are carrying in your heart. Offense will literally kill you if you continue to hold on to grudges, un-forgiveness, and anger towards those that hurt you. Offense causes stress in your body, and we all know that stress kills. So, is it worth it?

Do not play Russian Roulette with your life. Expose the spirit of offense and allow God to deliver you. Right now, you may be thinking, *"I hear you Patrea, but how do I get delivered and disarm these enemies of my soul*? I am so glad you asked me. We are now going to look into disarming the enemy.

How to Disarm the Enemy?

Now that we have had the chance to unmask various types of demonic spirits that can destroy the plans and purpose on your life, it is time for some soul searching. It is time to get real with where you are right now. God can not heal what you pretend to be, or what you refuse to reveal.

You have to be open, honest, and upfront about where you are right now. There is no reason to feel ashamed, guilty, or even embarrassed about where you are. If you can honestly say to yourself, Lord, I need Your help. Then this is a good thing. You are in a good place for healing and deliverance. So, what is deliverance? I'm sure many of you may know, but for those who may not—I will tell you.

Deliverance is the state of being saved from a painful or bad experience[25]: a setting free[26]

It is being liberated from pain, turmoil, torment, and demonic oppression. How is this done? It's initiated through our faith that God can and will deliver, and it is followed by the action of our faith by audibly confessing sin, repenting, and asking God to step in and free us. In the deliverance process, we stand on the Word of God as an absolute.

Every other idea, suggestion, or imagination other than the Word of God—we enforce our authority and by the act of our will—we choose to come out of agreement with interpersonal vows and allegiance with Satan and his cohorts.

Along with repenting of our sins, we also have to be willing to receive forgiveness. The most important, potent, and effective way of disarming the enemy is forgiveness. However, it can be easier at times to forgive others of their offenses, but often times we have a hard time forgiving ourselves. Can I take the opportunity to give you permission to let yourself off the hook? It is okay, to let yourself walk free from your past mistakes, your poor decision making, and any other baggage you may have picked up along the way. It's time to forgive and move on to the next great thing in your life. Your bright future awaits you.

Power of Forgiveness

"Then Peter came to Him and said, "Lord, how often shall my brother sin against me, and I forgive him? Up to seven times?" Jesus said to him, "I do not say to you, up to seven times, but up to seventy times seven." Matthew 18:21-22 NKJV [27]

We have all come to the place called "valley of decision". Each of us has had to deal with things or had to accept things that at one time or another hurt us, broke us, enraged us, disappointed us, blindsided us, and dang near completely derailed us. I mean the list goes on and on. Like I've stated before, I'm not in any way trying to diminish or minimize what may have happened to you, or even what you may be dealing with right now. I just strongly believe that we have to pull ourselves to the place of total and complete healing. To do this we must choose to forgive and walk in forgiveness even when it's in a tight place.

I know it's easier said than done, but forgiveness is the key that allows every door to open on your behalf. When you choose not to forgive, it is detrimental to your growth and your well-being. It's like that old saying, *"you are drinking poison in hopes that the other person will die".* When a person continues on with an unforgiving heart, they are constantly tormented by the thoughts of what their offender has done. The focus is hurt, and how to get even with them. Functioning with an unforgiving heart is also hard work. It takes a conscious decision to hold on to grudges and to hold on to hate. Listen, it is a total waste of time.

When we understand that there is power in forgiveness, life seems just a little bit sweeter. The power of forgiveness causes anger to dissipate, wounds to heal, doors to open, opportunities to emerge, blessings to be released, and gives internal peace. The power of forgiveness even causes our Heavenly Father to forgive us for our faults. It turns our focus from the other person and puts our focus on more important things.

This unforgiving spirit causes us to waste time and miss out on our blessings. It destroys our health and prevents us from cultivating healthy relationships. When you choose to forgive, you are freeing others, too. Forgiveness has everything to do with you, but when you do it…those who see you operating out of this new level of forgiveness will be inspired, and they will do the same. There is power in our forgiveness.

Jesus' love is the catalyst for forgiveness. It is by grace and the love of Jesus Christ that we are able to forgive. It is our love for Him that allows us to loosen the grips of the offense that held us captive. God said that we are to forgive seventy times seventy. That's a lot, right? He will grace us to do it, and He is able to take those bruised and broken places and make them whole again. Food for thought; "You are equipped with power when you forgive".

"Forgiveness is the very spirit of Heaven removing the hiding places of demonic activity from the caverns of the human soul. It is every wrong made right and every evil made void. The power of release in forgiveness is actually a mighty weapon in the war to save our cities." ~ Francis Frangipane

Here are some more effective ways to disarm the enemy. We can disarm and regain our victory through the Word of God, prayer, and worship. Now, let me be clear on this. There are going to be times where you are going to have to keep asking and keep standing on the Word of God. Remember, God is not a genie. He is God who knows, who sees, and who hears. He is a Father, who like most parents, knows what's best for us, and knows just what we need.

He cannot be manipulated. However, it's something about our faith that moves His heart. We see it all through scripture God, even our big brother Jesus always responded to faith. Without it, we can't please Him. [28] So, use your faith coupled with these weapons of destruction.

The Word of God

The word of God is our weapon of defense. It stands on its own and is living and active. When we truly understand the power of scripture, we will become more consistent with reading it, studying it, and dissecting it. We must eat the scroll of God's word. The Word of God is medicine to our bones. (*Read Proverbs 4:20-22*) It is imperative that we study the Word of God. The Word of God defeats the enemy. (Read Matthew 4:1-11, Joshua 1:8 NKJV) The Word of God defends you, protects you, sustains you, prepares you, and empowers you.

Why? Because it's inspired by God. *"All Scripture is given by inspiration of God, and is profitable for doctrine, for reproof, for correction, for [a]instruction in righteousness, that the man of God may be complete, thoroughly equipped for every good work."* 2 Timothy 3:16-17(NKJV)[29]

The Word of God is powerful enough to cut the enemy in half. God's Word is living. *"For the word of God is living and powerful, and sharper than any two-edged sword, piercing even to the division of soul and spirit, and of joints and marrow, and is a discerner of the thoughts and intents of the heart."* Hebrews 4:12 (NKJV)[30]

However, the only way this powerful weapon can work on your behalf is if you believe it, stand on it, proclaim it, confess it, and live by it. Demons can't and won't stand a chance if you do these things faithfully.

Prayer Is Everything

When you have been marked by fire, it is essential to have an intimate—active prayer life. We are marked to become partners with God to do great exploits with and for Him. In the following pages, you will find some powerful prayers that will jump-start you on your prayer journey.

Prayer is a key component of our growth and advancement, and without it, we are lost. The enemy has an advantage over us when we lack in prayer. Prayer will disarm the enemies of our souls, because when we pray; well, I believe when we pray, God leans down and invades our space and covers us in the glory of His presence.

Also, when we pray, God's presence illuminates and shines a light on every dark place giving us an advantage over our enemy. If we open ourselves up to Him, He will flood our very being with the light of His glory; causing everything that's not like Him to drop off of us. When we ask in faith God answers us as it states in Mark 11:24, *"Therefore I tell you, whatever you ask in prayer, believe that you have received it, and it will be yours."*[31]

The devil knows that when we're in the presence of God it's over for him, so he'll bring distractions, feelings of inadequacies, unbelief, and doubt. He'll try to lure us away by tricking us into believing that God doesn't hear our prayers, but this is an absolute lie for the pit of hell. God hears us when we call on Him.

> *"The Lord is near to all who call upon Him, to all who call upon Him in truth. He will fulfill the desire of those who fear Him; He also will hear their cry and save them. The Lord preserves all who love Him, But all the wicked He will destroy."* Psalm 145:18-20 NKJV [32]

When we call on God in truth and in reverence, He draws near to us, fills our desires, hears our cries, preserves us, saves us, and destroys our enemies. This is what happens when we pray. The only thing that will separate us from God or cause Him to hide His face from us when we pray is sin. *"But your iniquities have separated you from your God; and your sins have hidden His face from you, So that He will not hear."* Isaiah 59:2 NKJV[33]

This is why we must confess our sins, repent, and pray. We can't disarm the enemy if we grant him access. We must be sober when pray. We must be vigilant. *"Be [a]sober, be [b]vigilant; [c]because your adversary the devil walks about like a roaring lion, seeking whom he may devour."* 1 Peter 5:8 NKJV[34]

When we pray—hell gets nervous. Prayer is an honor and privilege—it should never be a task or an obligation. This how the enemy entangles us by using our fleshly desires. You know what I mean. *"Lord, I will pray tomorrow. I'm too tired to pray. I don't have time to pray—I'll just pray on my way to work instead."* I get it, trust me…I totally get it, but if we're trying to defeat the strong man (demonic spirit) we must pray. It's our first line of defense. When we pray, we receive instructions, insight, and the mind of God.

Prayer allows us to connect and hear what the Father has to say, how He feels, and what He wants to do in us, through us, and around us. It is written in 1 Thessalonians 5:16-18 that we are to *"rejoice always, pray without ceasing, and in everything give thanks; for this is the will of God in Christ Jesus for you."*[35]

Being marked by fire requires sacrifice in prayer. The only way we will truly understand who we are, what we're called to do, and how to disarm the enemies in our lives and in the lives of those connected to us is through prayer and supplication. There is no way around it…well…there is but, God's hand will not be in it, we'll still be bound, and eventually everything will fall apart. Trust me I know this firsthand, and oh, how much time I wasted. But I digress…

It is my earnest prayer and desire that when you look into the prayers written between the chapter sections and in the back of this book, the fire of the Holy Spirit will ignite your heart, stir your spirit, give you hope, encourage your heart, and set you on FIRE.

Prayer will cause you to stand even when you want to fall apart. *"The LORD will cause your enemies who rise against you to be defeated before your face; they shall come out against you one way and flee before you seven ways."* Deuteronomy 28:7 NKJV[36]

PRAYER WILL DISARM THE ENEMIES OF OUR SOULS…

Relentless Worship

For as long as I can remember, I loved singing, writing, and putting on a show. My dream as a little girl was to be a superstar! I look back at those days now, and I smile. There were no restraints. I was in my element, and the world was my oyster! All the pain around me would fade into the background. I enjoyed and loved the feeling of making people feel good while I sang to them. When hearing my cousins singing the songs that I wrote, it made me feel like I had something to offer. My goodness...I could write and sing for hours. I would get lost in my writing, and time stood still.

One Christmas my daddy bought me a karaoke machine and a 12 pack of 60-minute cassette tapes for me to record my songs on. Day in and out I would write, sing, and record. I did this so much that I would record over the songs that I recorded the day before. Music was my way of expressing how I felt when dealing with something tuff or just a creative avenue of release.

I did not understand back then that God was developing and shaping the craft of worship through writing and singing on the in me. So, when I was exposed to the arts of worship through singing and dance in ministry, it became my safe place. I was able to sing out to God my woes. I was able to write out my pains, and I was able to encourage myself and others through the Word of God through song. I didn't know that one day God would use my passion for music to bless His name. I didn't know that I would be a part of God's special selection of songstress (Prophetic Palmist) in the Earth that would declare His glory! God was refining me to be a skilled, sharp, polished instrument for battle in worship, at an incredibly young age. I'm still amazed, honored, and humbled in my spirit to partner with the God of the universe.

I'm sharing all this because I know God has marked me for worship! I'm known mostly from my stance in worship. The funny thing about that is...when I started to sing in the church as a young adult…fear tried paralyzed me. I was terrified to lead any song or even sing on command acapella, but I was okay with singing in the background. So, what happens? That little girl who was once free like a bird had become a caged bird.

However, God had other plans to break that caged bird out by giving me the courage to sing again freely and unapologetically. Little by little, and bit by bit, I had gotten more comfortable singing openly.   It was crazy that all those years as a child, loving to sing, and expressing my personality while doing it—I would find myself ashamed and scared! The devil is something else I tell you! Anyway, later on in life, I understood why the devil was trying his best to paralyze me in the area of creativity, singing, and writing; because he knew what was awaiting me in the near future. He knew that worship would become my signature. He knew that worship would be the choicest weapon in my arsenal that I would cause his kingdom destruction! My worship would be the onslaught, and the most important tool I had to use against the attacks against me.

Worship creates an atmosphere that produces freedom! It creates a sound of warning to the kingdom of darkness and a sound that reverberates throughout the earth! Worship is more than just singing a song or getting an emotional rush, but it is a demonstration of our love towards God openly! It is more than the instruments playing in our sanctuaries, or the instrumentals song we may play in our homes from YouTube. Worship is a sound! Yes! A sound of freedom. A sound of victory!

A sound of gratefulness to God. Worship is a sound of surrender and a response to God's presence. Worship is a sound of faith. It is a sound that says, "God I still trust You and believe." Worship is a sound…yes. Worship and praise is a weapon that will confuse and ambush our enemy. Psalm 149:6 says, *"Let the high praise of God be in their mouth, and a two-edge sword in their hand."*[37]

"When we worship and praise God, it's like we begin to wage war against all that is wrong, with a two-edge sword."[38] ~ Tim Hughes

We can find a variety of examples throughout scripture that shows us the true power of worship. For example, when Paul and Silas worshipped—the chains broke, and the prison doors opened. When King Jehoshaphat had a multitude of armies against him—when he began worshipping, the enemy turned on themselves.

"Worship changes our perspective. It lifts the attention off ourselves, our problems, our limited and fragile thinking and shifts it on to the unshakable, faithful and all-powerful provision of our God." [39] ~ Tim Hughes

Relentless worship disarms the enemies of our souls because it says, *"We do not know what to do but our eyes are on you."* 2 Chronicles 20:12$_b$[40] Worship is a surrender of life to the Father and an open show of commitment to Him. Worship is a place of humility and vulnerability before our God.

Worship literally saved my life! There was a time when I became suicidal, and I thought about the story of David and Saul. Saul would call for David to minister to him on the harp in times of his distress so that he could be at peace. Read 1 Samuel 16:14-23

So, during that dark moment. I sat on my bed with pen and paper in hand, and I began to write these lyrics, *"Lord, it's me again, I need you now please listen. My heart is overwhelmed it seems like life is crumbling. Lord why, oh my, not this again—not this again. I just want to love You. A life dedicated to serve you, but doublemindedness won't do; so take Your place again. You are Alpha and Omega, take Your place again, You are Author and Finisher, take Your place again—Strong Deliverer—breakthrough and shatter every wall I need you!"* ~Patrea Brumfield

You see, worship brings an awareness of our frailties and the need for God to step in! It is a mark on our lives that lets hell know that we belong to the King of all kings! And, when we open our mouths, or dance our dance, or play our instruments, or pray or prayers—God the Creator of heaven and Earth will respond and fight for us! Worship is our signature—our MARK!

Consistent Obedience

I provided you with a list of crucial weapons to assist with disarming the enemy. This last weapon is a MUST have in order to effectively maintain your freedom...this weapon is "Consistent Obedience". Consistent obedience is what keeps all the other weapons engaged. This weapon is the foundation of them all, and also the weapon that sets all the other weapons in motion.

Without consistent obedience to God, all the listed weapons to disarm the devil is pointless! Our submission and obedience to God and His Word will always cause the enemy to turn back and flee! *"Therefore submit to God. Resist the devil and he will flee from you."*[41] I love this piece of scripture because it enlightens our understanding of the benefits we acquire when we submit ourselves to God. Our obedience should draw us closer to God. *"Draw near to God and He will draw near to you. Cleanse your hands, you sinners; and purify your hearts, you double-minded."*[42]

You see not only do our obedience draw us to God and God to us, but there is a requirement with this interaction. "REQUIREMENT"... Yes, requirement. Weapons require practices, guidance, study, instruction, and active participation to develop the skill to handle them all. It requires us to remain holy, to stay purified in our hearts, and requires us to be solid in our minds. Consistent obedience supersedes sacrifice and performance it is the most potent antidote in our arsenal that will make the devil fall back each time!
Read this what the Word of God has to say about it...

"So Samuel said: "Has the Lord as great delight in burnt offerings and sacrifices, As in obeying the voice of the Lord? Behold, to obey is better than sacrifice, And to heed than the fat of rams. For rebellion is as the sin of witchcraft, And stubbornness is as iniquity and idolatry. Because you have rejected the word of the Lord, He also has rejected you from being king." [43] 1 Samuel 15:22-22 (NKJV)

So, if you want to disarm the enemy and want to make him back up off you then FORGIVE, STUDY THE WORD, PRAY, WORSHIP, BE CONSISTENT IN OBEYING GOD, AND REPEAT.

Let us Pray:

Heavenly Father,
I just want to take this moment to say thank You for Your grace and Your loving kindness towards me. Thank You for gracing me to forgive even when it hurts. Father, I choose to obey Your Word. I choose to forgive those who hurt me, those who have wronged me, those who have betrayed me, and those who have slandered my name. Lord, I choose to be kindhearted, compassionate and forgiving just as You have forgiven me. (Ephesians 4:32) Father, I choose to forgive by the power and act of my will. Today, I make an exchange with You. I exchange my broken and bruised heart, for a new heart—a heart that can love, a heart that is filled with joy, and a heart that can forgive. Help me to set free (insert name(s) of those who offend you or hurt you here). Lord, I release them into Your hands now. Lord, help me to go through the process of forgiveness. Help me to walk in love, righteousness, peace, faithfulness, consistency, and determination that demonstrates Your power within me. In Jesus Christ's Name, Amen.

Recovery Room

When we began to dismantle, expose, and disarm the enemy, we will find damage that requires some attention. We will find that we need healing, love, and care. We will also find that we are fragile, and we will need to be handled with care. The healing process is necessary for the assignment that is on your life. Spiritually, if you don't heal then you will not fulfill God's purpose and calling on your life. If you do not allow yourself to heal, you will abort the assignment, you will forfeit the call on your life, and returning to old patterns of behavior. What comes to mind when you hear the word "Recovery?" You may say, "Recuperation" or "having something stolen recovered", or something similar. When I think of recovery, I think of someone who has undergone surgery and reconstruction and needs rest. Oftentimes God "The Doctor of doctors" lets us know that we need to undergo surgery in order for us to function appropriately.

Sometimes, we may feel as though we need a second opinion, but God knows that there is a definite need for a heart transplant. Even though undergoing surgery may leave the patient in extreme pain after the operation, the transplant is extremely necessary and oftentimes painful. When a person is informed that they require surgery, the doctor usually provides them with certain instructions to prepare. The doctor informs them of their condition, what's needs to be done to correct the problem, pre-operation procedures, and post-operation procedures. Usually, surgery is needed when something serious is occurring within the body. Sometimes things have to be removed, bones have to be realigned, organs have to be replaced, and/or valves have to be redirected. Some surgeries even require bones to be broken during surgery to cast your body anew. Where am I going with this, you may ask? Sometimes God has to break us in order to heal us. He breaks us to mold us, position us, and restore us. Whatever the case, the surgery has a purpose. There is purpose in the pain. In the recovery room pain is necessary. Yes, you read that right. In this case, pain is considered a sign of healing, and it is a key indicator that the body is getting better. Eventually, we begin to look better, feel better, become better, take care of ourselves better, function better, and we become more aware. The pain and complications are no longer there. The recovery room is just that "recovery" a place to recover and to regain. In the recovery room, you get back your strength, your faith is stirred, your hope renewed, and most importantly you heal. Embrace the surgery and embrace the recovery. Afterall deliverance, recovery, and rebounding are vital because if we're not careful we can be pulled and drawn back to the very thing that trapped us in the beginning.

Let us Pray:

Heavenly Father,
I thank You for being my healer, deliverer, and restorer. Lord, I am willing to go through spiritual surgery, and I ask You Lord for a new heart. Take away any and everything that offends You. Take away any and everything that is contrary to Your word, to Your ways, to Your Kingdom agenda. Lord, open me up and remove anything that is not like You. Your Word says that when we ask in faith; You are faithful to answer me. Lord, I'm ready... Do what You will. I trust that I will recover in the palm of Your hand, and rest in Your safety. Heal me, O Lord, and I will be healed; save me and I will be saved, for You are the one I praise". Jeremiah 17:14[44]

In Jesus Christ's Name, Amen.

PART II
CHOSEN ONE

Chapter 3

Born Identity

"Thus says the Lord, your Redeemer, and He who formed you from the womb: "I am the Lord, who makes all things, who stretches out the heavens all alone, who spreads abroad the earth by Myself. Isaiah 44:24 New King James Version (NKJV)

Who are you? Do you truly know who you are? I'm not talking about the many different roles that you fill or the titles that you uphold. At your core, who are you, really? If there's a hesitation or you draw a blank then this chapter will provide insight, and it will empower you with knowledge and encouragement and point you in the right direction of who you have been marked to be. Let's walk through this journey of identity.

This chapter was the most challenging for me to write. It required raw honesty, reflection, growth, and maturity. I had to reflect, draft, edit, and revise. The topic of identity has such depth in its own right. I may barely scratch the surface, but I'm sure you'll get what you need. I'm going to take this moment to share my personal revelations as I was learning the walk of "identity. I will give you my thoughts and also provide you with some additional resources, should you want to delve a little deeper into this topic. Let's jump in—shall we!

Identity describes who you are, the way you think about yourself, how others view you, and all of the characteristics that define you. If we don't embrace our true identity and know who we are, then we become vulnerable and fall prey to the opinions of others. We'll quickly buy into the lies of the enemy.

Embracing our born identity is imperative. We can tell how quintessential it is because He within scripture God communicates who we are, and how He calls us by name, and that He knows us. (Look at Isaiah 44:24, Psalm 71:6, Galatians 1:15) Furthermore, Prophet Jeremiah was told by God in Jeremiah 1:5, "Before I formed thee in the belly I knew thee; and before thou camest forth out of the womb. I sanctified thee, and I ordained thee a prophet unto the nations."[45] Right then God told Jeremiah who he (Jeremiah) was. Jeremiah was created and identified as being ordained by God as a prophet before he was formed in his mother's womb. However, Jeremiah's view of himself was not aligned with who God created him to be. Look at Jeremiah's response to God.

"Ah, Lord GOD. Behold, I cannot speak: for I am a child."
Jeremiah 1:6 NKJV

Refuting Jeremiah's perception of himself, God comes back and says to Jeremiah,

> "But the LORD said unto me, Say not, I am a child: for thou shalt go to all that I shall send thee, and whatsoever I command thee thou shalt speak. Be not afraid of their faces: for I am with thee to deliver thee, saith the LORD. Then the LORD reached out His hand, touched my mouth, and said to me: "Behold, I have put My words into your mouth. See, I have appointed you today over nations and kingdoms to uproot and tear down, to destroy and overthrow, to build and plant." Jeremiah 1:7-10[46]

God affirmed and confirmed Jeremiah's purpose and who He created Jeremiah to be for the second time, but the second time God spoke, He provided Jeremiah with more detail. He took away Jeremiah's excuses. He had clear and concise information regarding Jeremiah's identity and Jeremiah had to choose to accept it.

When something is named, it now has an identity. Yes, when we give a name to something, we give it an identity. This is what happened in the garden when Adam began to name the animals. That's why when we hear or see a "lion" we know what to identify, because of its name. Powerful right? God downloads things inside of us and then He names us in accordance with our purpose.

You see before my encounter at the altar, everything warred against the image and the name of God spoke concerning me. That night I had to decide. Just like Jeremiah, I had to choose whether to trust and believe what God was saying about me or believe what the devil was speaking to me. If we're going to be everything that God has called us to be, we must have strong identity roots. In order to be everything God has purposed us to be, we must be willing to target our weaknesses, maximize our strengths; master our crafts, and all while transforming our minds with the Word of God. (Read Roman 12: 2)

We have been created and identified in love. We have been created and identified with purpose. We have been created and identified with immeasurable possibilities. We have been created and identified with certainty. God infuses us with abilities, qualities, visions, dreams, intellect, gifts, talents, solutions, personalities, and creativity. God knew that wouldn't be enough, so He added to us grace, mercy, faith, strength, power, discernment, character, and the power of choice... the will. We have an option to choose.

When God marks us, He identifies us, and he establishes us. But, if we're to truly understand our identity then we must embrace that it can be a daunting learning experience. Understanding our identity and knowing who we are can be overwhelming. Having a true knowledge of identity can be complex and broad. Since my encounter with God years back, I've been on a quest to gain more understanding of my identity.

This is where my experienced author friend makes his debut. If you are intrigued and have a desire to know more about your true identity from a Christian perspective then the book "Who God Says You Are A Christian Understanding of Identity" by Klyne R Snodgrass will get you on the right track.

Of course, we are all recognized and identified by our physical appearance. If you know me you can identify me by my features, my voice, and my mannerisms. You can pick me out of the crowd. That's a form of identity.

Our history shapes our identities. You've heard of the phrase, "you are a product of your environment." It's a very true statement. Yes, we can learn how to undo some behavior, but we can't erase history. The records of our lives shape our identities, and there is no separation.

That history is a part of us no matter how great or no matter how terrible; that history is attached to our identities. For example, if a child has a brother who set a house on fire by accident, and the fire killed an entire family, then that child's mother, father, siblings, and other family members are tied to that history because that situation inevitably is tied to the name of that person, and his family members. They can't change what happened, thus they are identified by the history of it.

We are also identified by our relationships, our commitment, and other things too. Identity unfortunately is also given by people. There is no escaping it. When we are born, our parents typically name us giving us our natural identity, but God gives us our spiritual identity before either of parents suspect our arrival. He's awesome, right?

So, with identities taking on so many different forms, we can find ourselves getting lost in transition. If I were to ask a woman the question, "Who are you?" She may quickly respond, "I am a mother, sister, wife, business-woman, pastor, teacher, a baker, etc." Her identity would be based on her roles in relationships, and what she does in them. Here's another example. If a singer only identifies themselves as just a singer, and in their ability to sing then if something traumatic were to happen to them causing them to lose their voice then their identity would also be lost as well; because their identity would be rooted and shaped by their abilities and what they were known to do; sing.

Likewise, if a person's identity is only found in their relationships after the relationship has ended, that person's identity would also be lost. You see, whatever identifies a person, becomes their life source. Let us take a look at some identity barriers that we come up against when we pull back the layers when learning our true identities.

Types of Identity Barriers

What would happen if our identities were only found in what we did well or what we do? What would happen if we couldn't "do" those things anymore or no longer function in the same role? What if what we did well no longer received appreciation anymore? What would happen if our identities were based on the greatest season of our lives, and a new season started with a losing streak? Who would we be? What would we be? God has revealed to me some barriers I've struggled with throughout my life over the years. I'm going to share a few of the concepts with you.

After much research, I discovered that our identities can be based on a variety of things such as our relationships, our history, our commitments, our careers, our environments, our physical appearance, and a multitude of other factors. However, in the cluster of things that provide us with identity. I didn't know that perception of others similarly shapes our identity.

So of course, these factors resonated with me. I have

titled the identity barriers "influenced-based". Influence has a lot to do with the conformity of our identities and forms our views.

Influence is having the capacity to have an effect on the character, development, or behavior of someone or something, or the effect itself; the power to shape policy or ensure favorable treatment from someone, especially through status, contacts, or wealth; a person or thing with the capacity or power to have an effect on someone or something.[47] Whatever is attached to that influence is what determines and distinguishes our identity.

I. Relationship-Influenced Identity Barrier

Over the years, my identity issues stemmed from a relationship-influence base and any social circles that would accept me. I would morph into those around me. What's so dangerous about relationship-influenced base identity is a person gives over their rights to another to determine who they were created to be; by a person who didn't create themselves. It's basically living out how others desire us to be, leaving us without our own thoughts or our opinions. We've seen this before.

Ex. A mother desires her son to be just like his father, so she puts pressure on him to take on the family business and run it exactly like his father. The son responds to customers as his father, frames all of his ideas like he believes his father would, dresses like his father, and behaves like his father.

If the son wishes to please his mom, he will eventually compromise his own identity to salvage the relationship. The son will now function from a relationship-influenced identity. His identity is rooted based on his relationship with his mother, and not who God created him to be. A relationship-influenced base identity will cause the person to conform rather than be to their true authentic selves for the sake of the relationship.

What would happen if the person who allowed others to control them no longer met the expectations of that relationship, or if the relationship ended? Who would they be? If the person stops receiving their identity to the one suggesting ideas and opinions, who would they be? Relationship-influenced identity is grounded in the need to be accepted and validated by someone other than God.

Relationship-influenced identity tends to stroke the ego of the person who doesn't truly know themselves. Their identity is rooted in the defectiveness of the codependent relationship, so they don't evaluate the possibility of being of value to someone else or to a greater purpose. Instead, they settle for the attention of now; instead of letting go and embracing relationships that cultivate growth, development, cohesiveness, community, and love.

This is why it is important to surround ourselves with people who are solid in their identity and trustworthy. Allowing them to hold us accountable for our own self-discovery. Looking to others for our identities is an epic fail. Yes, our identities are shaped by relationships, but that's just one piece of the puzzle. That's why it's crucial to maintain a healthy identity.

Seasons change within relationships and if our identities are wrapped in those relationships when that season ends, we will have nothing to sustain us. Also, when we look to those relationships to determine our value it becomes problematic because if those people don't value us, we'll believe we have nothing of value.

I heard a sermon years ago that was titled "A twenty is a twenty no matter whose hands it flowed through." The moral of the sermon, God gives us our identity and He establishes our value. No matter what relationships changed, how we were mishandled, or despite our flawed view of ourselves; our value does not CHANGE. Our identities do not CHANGE.

II. Success-Influenced Identity Barrier

I struggled here before too. Those who are driven by success-influenced base identity battle with perfectionism, competition, overachievement, and comparison. This is barrier describes someone who bases who they are on their overall accomplishments and success. In doing so, they will never come into their true God-given identity.

Those who base their identities in success will try to hide their born identity behind their success, and they will only attribute their identity to how they've succeeded in accomplishing a goal or in the promotion they've received. Their achievements make them "feel" important. If they've not accomplished anything, reached a certain level of success, received homage, or the accolades then they feel as though they are worthless.

Outside of their success, this person will wander through life looking for acknowledgment, applause, praise, esteem, recognition, and validation from others based on their accomplishments. However, if they are lacking success then they are lacking sustenance. Now, it is great attaining education and bettering ourselves by expanding our knowledge, but that's not all of who we are. As aforementioned, it's just one piece of the puzzle. There is more to us. So much more.

Unfortunately, the success-influenced identity drives individuals through live life thinking they know who they are, only to find out years later that they wasted years of being someone they were not. They begin to realize they were actually living below God's standard of who He called them to be. I have been here so many times. I thought that I would be loved more, or accepted if I did more, achieved more, or gained more. Unfortunately, I had to find out the hard way—all of that was not enough, and sadly—it tore me apart. Our identities are not found in our successes. IT'S JUST A PIECE OF THE PUZZLE.

So many individuals wrestle with this next barrier. This barrier can cause trauma and insecurity; and depending on the severity of the anguish can even cause some to take their own lives. Relationships and marriages are afflicted by this barrier. This barrier is the Social Media Influenced Identity.

III. Social Media Influenced Identity Barrier

Social media influenced identity is an identity rooted in the connectivity or interaction of others on a social media outlet or forum. I would consider this barrier the worst of them all. Although, social media platforms serve as a positive way to keep others connected, as of late it seems to influence in more ways negative. Growing up we may see someone who possesses qualities that we admire in hindsight. However, we face a different reality. We see everything that we admire with one stroke of a finger. If we're not careful that admiration will lead to comparison, jealousy, and covetousness.

Likewise, if we're not careful then a false reality will dictate how we feel we should be loved based on how others show their love or affirm one another on social media platforms. If we lack that kind of attention; we will start to determine our value-based on how someone liked, tweeted, commented, or posted on their pages about someone else or on another person's page.

When we do not know our true identity and value—we will always look for it outside of God and outside of ourselves. Social media platforms can be a blessing and also a curse. Why? Because it gives us a platform to share how and what we feel at any given moment. It can become our little "g" god in some instances. We'll look for people to give us that sense of validation and security.

While there is nothing wrong with being acknowledged by others, we cannot unravel when we feel we aren't receiving the social praise from strangers that we deserve. God made us relational. We all desire connectivity, and we all desire to fit in and belong, right? But, at what price? If I were to rate your sales value, what would your value be? We advertise how much we are in hopes that we're appealing to those viewing our posts, tweets, or snaps. Their false appraisals can never measure up to the authenticity and immeasurable value God has downloaded inside of you! For whatever reason, the social media-influenced identity is falsely established from the number of likes, retweets, and followers. If those things only determine who we are. Then who are we really?

Our identities must not get lost in the fickleness of the opinions and influences of people behind their screen. Social media is a mirage. We only see who people post to be. In a recent article from Psychology Today, titled "How Honest Are People on Social Media," the author discovered that social media sites breed grounds for dishonesty. The author stated that "humans are naturally social creatures, and crave for relationship and interaction,"[4] which speaks to my statement of God making us relational. When given platforms such as Facebook, Instagram, and Twitter, given our social nature to desire connectivity, we often get our wires crossed. Our identities cannot be rooted and based on the responses we receive from these different platforms. No matter the number of followers, if we don't know who we are outside of these social media platforms, then who are we really?

If our identity is based on social media approval and how others respond to our posts, then we measure who we are on the basis of others. We have to nip it in the bud, especially if we start to feel depressed or find ourselves in a constant battle of comparison to other peoples' news feeds or threads. I will venture to say that our identity has been compromised if this is happening, and self-evaluation must be conducted immediately. We can be so consumed by trying to look the part, play the role, and out-perform others that we become lost in the chaos and eventually lose ourselves.

Listen, I've been here too. No judgment. Throughout these chapters, you will see the phrase "I've been there", repeatedly, but it's the truth. Social media almost crushed me. My identity was lost in this false sense of reality. I felt like if no one liked my pictures, comments, or tagged me into their post then I was not a person of relevance. If I posted a comment that did not garner replies, then I felt like I didn't have anything of value to say. It was like social media enhanced my insecurities. It served as a false validation of true loyalty, love, support, and friendship from others—an outright mirage.

Sadly, I determined how people showed up for me over the airwaves seemed to conclude the prominence of their love and concern for me. Even though that was not always the case; my belief about it was so deep-rooted in this jaded certainty and the only thing I had anchoring my identity and my relevance. IT WAS A TRAP, and I fell for it! **DON'T TAKE THE BAIT**

Even if you don't get what you need for those on social media outlets, or if you have voice those needs to that person or persons on how it makes you feel. Understand this, you can't control others or what they do on their personal forums, but it is, however, your responsibility to control and govern yourself, your emotions, and maintain a healthy thought life for yourself. I've learned if a person doesn't consider how certain things impact you or take it into consideration of how it makes you feel, then maybe they're not for you.

Even if this is or isn't the case, it still doesn't take away from who you are as a person. Your identity should not be rooted in their social opinion about you anyway. Make note of their actions and keep moving forward. Don't lose yourself or your identity...especially to those who show no concern. Trust me, it is not worth it. You have to remember you have so much to give and to offer even if it may go unrecognized over the airways. It's just another piece...

IV. Work -Influenced Identity Barrier

Lastly, we have the work-influenced identity. In a male-dominated world, I believe this is an area of struggle for men. Men who are raised to be the breadwinners, protectors and providers for their families often lose their identities in their workload. If they are hardworking and providing for their families, society establishes them as a good "MAN".
Their work ethic influences their identities as men who are great, loving, and caring. But that is far from the truth.

Likewise, women also have this complex. Especially, our minority women. We believe that if we work exceedingly hard then we are identified as strong, independent *go-getters*; but the truth of the matter is no matter how much we work, it still does not determine or define our identities. What we do for a living (job or career) is just another piece of the identity puzzle, and it is not absolute.

Our true identities are only found in Jesus Christ and based upon the spoken Word of God. (Read Psalms 139). I'm fully persuaded that people struggling with weak identities will have a hard time developing relationships, exploring new opportunities, or trying new things. They base who they are on everything outside of themselves and have not yet sought out who they are from the One who created them in the first place.

We have to be aware of the barriers that infect our perception of our true identity. A self-evaluation should always be in session. If you are struggling in your identity, I ask that you take this moment to ask the Holy Spirit to remove all false identities, barriers, and facades that you have acquired. Ask Him to expose root causes and reestablish your new identity. Please jot down in your journal or on a piece of paper those things that He reveals, so that you will be able to recognize any triggers during the process of yourself-discovery.

I'll leave you with this: We are born to rule, we are peculiar, and we are sealed with a promise, appointed, and touched by the finger of God. Stand in that, and embrace your true God-given identity found in Christ alone.

Wounded Identity

For years I struggled in my identity. It took me a long time, and I'm still processing through some things (I am a work in progress). When I was lived my life by the rules of the world, my struggle with identity didn't seem as evident. Why? Because my identity was rooted in everything surrounding me, I couldn't differentiate how poor and damaged my identity was.

But, something happens when we give our lives over to Christ. He begins to untie some things and shine His light on things that have been twisted and mangled for a very long time. See, when we give our lives to God our spirit becomes free. Although our spirits are free, habitually our souls (mind, will, and emotions) and our hearts remain in bondage. That's why deliverance is so important. If we are going to walk in our true identities, we must rid ourselves from the enemies of our souls that cripple our identity. What I discovered about identity is if the soul is wounded then our identity is also wounded. If we don't find the source of the wound, then the infection of it will continue to grow and cripple and blind us from seeing and receiving our true identity.

Wounds of the Soul—Damaged Identity

We have to understand the difference between a wounded soul or the act of our flesh. Typically, when we are dealing with an act of our flesh, we can easily bring whatever that thing is into subjection through prayer, by the act of our will (choice), the advice from a loved one or trusted friend, or through a change in our behavior. When we are operating in our flesh we tend to act out of character, but when our souls are wounded, we tend to react from the pain. Our response comes from the wound within our soul, and that's not something that can be easily corrected. A wound requires treatment, care, assistance, and attention to.

To act is to intentionally do something on and with purpose. You are in control of what you are doing. To *react* is an impulsive manner without control. It comes out without warning. You see, both don't equate. When we act, we have full control. We have a choice. When we react, there is no control. For instance, if you had a deep wound that required attention, you would go to the doctor where they would clean, medicate, stitch, and then wrap the wound. That doesn't mean the wound no longer hurts, right? So, you would proceed with caution. Though you are in the process of healing, you are still hurting. You guard that wound to make sure you don't bump it, graze it, or lay on it because it would hurt. We know right well that that wound is not going heal overnight, and that healing will take time.

With this in mind, if someone intentionally or unintentionally picks at your healing wound, you would have an instantaneous and impulsive reaction. You have no control over it; you didn't even have time to think about it—you just reacted. I'm not condoning poor behavior. I believe we are still responsible for holding ourselves and others accountable by seeking the proper help that is needed so that we're not walking around blowing up every time a wound is grazed or bumped. We just have to understand that some healing requires a longer period of recovery in others. The deeper the wound is the longer the recovery may be. Wounds are covered in so many different forms, so how can we recognize if we are wounded or not?

Let's start here. We are a three-part being. We have our physical body, spirit, and soul. Our physical bodies house the soul and spirit temporarily. However, our soul is the essence of who we are. The soul houses our mind, will, intellect, emotions, and personalities. It's our souls that give us our uniqueness. However, our spirit is what makes it possible for us to fellowship and communicate with God. If we are going to do anything productively for God, we must learn how to receive healing for our souls.

I recently read a powerful article from Katie Souza archived on her website katiesouza.com. She is a powerhouse, and well acquainted with wounds of the soul. She lives out of the revelation of dwelling among tombs. I'm going to share a part of her testimony that truly spoke to me and provided some of the inspiration for this chapter.

How Soul Wound Work- Part 3
By Katie Souza

"I have lived out the revelation of dwelling among the tombs and I am going to share with you how soul wounds work. In Oklahoma, I had a dream that I was cooking methamphetamines. However, I haven't done that for over a decade. God talks to us through our dreams and visions and I believe that He was showing me a big wound that had been formed in my soul from when I manufactured meth. I didn't know why He was telling me at that particular moment, but by faith and obedience, I moved on it. I repented for making meth and applied the blood of Jesus to the sin. Then I began to apply dunamis power to the wounds that sin had made. It took just fifteen minutes to get healed. Later, with my spiritual senses, I smelled chemicals that are used in cooking meth when I walked into the room I was to minister in. So, I spoke to the woman who was hosting the meeting, "I had a dream last night about cooking meth and now I can smell those chemicals. Do you know anything about that?" She said, "Yes – when we were first renting this building, we were told that this room had been used for a methamphetamine lab."

This is a whole new way to take dominion over the enemy. I needed dominion in that place. I could not have anything in my soul that was in common with demonic powers over that room, or I would not have the authority to do what I needed to do. So God showed me the wound in my soul, created by sin, which was attached to the demonic over that room; I got dominion, and signs and wonders broke out. You've been praying for your child and wondering why you have not been getting breakthrough. It's because they wounded your soul. They wounded your soul and you wounded theirs... There are demonic powers attached to those wounds that you both have in common. You are trying to kick that demon off of them and that demon is standing back going, "Oh, good luck with that. I'm on both of you.." You need to get your soul healed first.

The healing of your soul is directly connected to healing in your physical body and in your finances. "Beloved, I wish above all things that you may prosper (there's your finances) and be in health (there's your body), even as thy soul prospereth." 3 John 2 (KJV). Where is the miracle that you have been waiting for in your money? It's stored up in Heaven and it is going to come when you get your soul healed, because the wounds on your soul control every part of your being – your mind, your will and your emotions. If you got the blessing right now, soul wounds would control the way you think about the blessing and would control your emotions causing you to act fleshly and emotional. They would control your will – your ability to choose to do the right thing with the blessing. Also, the healing of your soul is directly connected to your physical health. Back-aches, neck-aches, diseases – all kinds of health issues- can manifest because there are wounds on our soul."

Powerful. Right? When I read that article, it made me rethink some beliefs about identity. As aforesaid, when we began to name a thing, we give that thing identity. We give it life. So, I wondered...what if the thing we identified is not exactly the thing (problem, root, or person) we think it is? We have committed a case of mistaken identity. Mistaken Identity- When someone incorrectly thinks that they have found or recognized a particular person.[48]

Wounds of the souls steal our identity, causing us to show anger, jealousy, pride, control, shame, fear, bitterness, and rejection. So sadly, those around us come to identify us with those things, and really, it's not us, but the wound taking over our identity.

Self-examination is crucial during these times. You must find the source of your emotional woundedness. Ask the Holy Spirit to reveal those areas to you. Ask the right questions.

- What caused this soul wound?
- Who or what caused this soul wound?
- How do I heal from this soul wound?
- How long have I had this soul wound?
- In what ways do or have I over-reacted out of this soul wound?
- What do I know to be the trigger of the soul wound?

These questions are just to help jump-start the investigation process. Remember to always seek out the assistance of the Holy Spirit. God said that he will restore and heal our wounds. "For I will restore health to you and heal you of your wounds,' says the Lord." Jeremiah 30:17a (NKJV)[49]

If you are the cause of your pain, repent, and ask the Lord for forgiveness. You have to understand that when you hold on to any remorse, guilt, bitterness, doubt, anger, shame, un-forgiveness, and self-imposed emotions; you have now allowed those wounds to become a stronghold within your mind. What happens when we allow this type of stronghold to take residence in our minds? We are actually creating a place where the enemy can come and go as he pleases, thus granting him access to control us at any time he wants. Satan dominates in our wounded areas. You need to demolish these strongholds with the truth of God's Word and by the power of the Holy Spirit. Declare your healing. Confess that you have already been healed by the stripes of Jesus. *"But He was wounded for our transgressions, He was bruised for our iniquities; the chastisement for our peace was upon Him, and by His stripes we are healed."* Isaiah 53:5 (NKJV)[50]

You must also forgive. You must forgive yourself and forgive those who have wounded your soul. You have to understand that when someone sins against you, they are not acting out of their own accord. Satan uses open wounds in people so that they can inflict pain against one another to divide, wound, and conquer using horrible schemes. When you take a step back and really, really, really, take a good focused look, you will find the influence of the devil every time you encounter a wound, strife, feelings of confusion or hatred, and anything associated with evil. Yes, we can see, hear, and touch those who hurt us, but they are not our actual enemy. *"For we do not wrestle against flesh and blood, but against principalities, against powers, against the rulers of the darkness of this age, against spiritual hosts of wickedness in the heavenly places."* Ephesians 6:12 (NKJV)[51]

Now, I'm not in any way trying to diminish or negate what that person may have done to you. I just sincerely want you to heal and walk into you place of freedom. If we don't forgive then the enemy will still have power over us. He doesn't fight fair, so he'll use those wounds to torment us. Sadly, when we don't forgive— our souls are turned over to the hands over the tormentor.

"Then Peter came to Him and said, "Lord, how often shall my brother sin against me, and I forgive him? Up to seven times?" Jesus said to him, "I do not say to you, up to seven times, but up to seventy times seven. Therefore, the kingdom of heaven is like a certain king who wanted to settle accounts with his servants. And when he had begun to settle accounts, one was brought to him who owed him ten thousand talents. But as he was not

able to pay, his master commanded that he be sold, with his wife and children and all that he had, and that payment be made. The servant therefore fell down before him, saying, 'Master, have patience with me, and I will pay you all.' Then the master of that servant was moved with compassion, released him, and forgave him the debt. "*But that servant went out and found one of his fellow servants who owed him a hundred denarii; and he laid hands on him and took him by the throat, saying, 'Pay me what you owe.'*

So his fellow servant fell down at his feet and begged him, saying, 'Have patience with me, and I will pay you all.' And he would not, but went and threw him into prison till he should pay the debt. So when his fellow servants saw what had been done, they were very grieved, and came and told their master all that had been done. Then his master, after he had called him, said to him, 'You wicked servant. I forgave you all that debt because you begged me. Should you not also have had compassion on your fellow servant, just as I had pity on you?' And his master was angry, and delivered him to the torturers until he should pay all that was due to him." Matthew 18:20-34 (NKJV)[52]

Not only are we tormented, but our Heavenly Father will not forgive us. "*But if you do not forgive men their trespasses, neither will your Father forgive your trespasses.*" Matthew 6:15 (NKJV)[53]

We have to give up our will in order to be healed. We have to give up our will to be right in order to be healed. When we give up our wills for us to take back our power to fulfill the purpose and destiny on our lives. When we do, we ultimately take back our true identities established and rooted in Jesus Christ.

Restored Identity

I just love hearing that word...R-E-S-T-O-R-E-D. Ooo-oooh, it refreshes my soul within. I'm blessed to say that

I've experienced God's divine restoration. Restored means to bring back (a previous right, practice, custom, or situation); reinstate; to return (someone or something) to a former condition, place, or position; to repair or renovate (a building, work of art, vehicle, etc.) so as to return it to its original condition.[54] Lord, have mercy! I can just dance my dance right there! When God restores us, He brings us back into our right place. God restores our identity. Think about that for a minute.

Here are some biblical descriptors of what our new identity in Christ secures for us:

He Loves Us – He loves us so much that He sacrificed His only Son (Jesus). **John 3:16**

He Selects Us – God calls us His own. **Isaiah 43:1**

He Justifies Us – He Marked by a good or legitimate reason.[55] **Romans 8:30**

He Purifies Us – He cleanses us with His Word **John 15:3**

He Regenerates Us – Imparting new spiritual life to us. "Born Again" **John 3:3**

He Adopts Us – We can call Him Abba. Father. **Romans 8:15**

He Predestinates Us – He establishes as His sons and daughters. **Ephesian 1:5**

He Propitiates Us – He rights our wrongs. **1 John 4:10**

He Redeems Us – He reconciles us and pays our ransom by His blood. **Colossians 1:20**

He Gives Us An Inheritance – Saved into the glorious riches of his grace. **Ephesians 1:11**

He Sanctifies Us – He washes with the truth of His word. **John 17:17**

He Glorifies Us – He makes us glorious by bestowing honor. **Romans 8:30**

He Saves and Calls Us – He gives purpose. **2 Timothy 1:9**

(SPEAK IT OUT LOUD)

AFFIRMATION- I have Identity

I am who God says I am. I am strong. I am wise. I am valued. There is only one me. I am unique. I have been chosen. I have been called, and I have been predestined. All of who I am; my identity, personality, and everything about me is robed into the identity of my Creator. I have been covered, designed, and established from the Words of my Father. He knows everything about me. I have nothing missing, nothing lacking, and nothing broken in me. My identity is found in Jesus Christ. My identity is secured in Jesus Christ. I am a child of the King, and He knows my name. I will not trade in who I am to be accepted by others.

I refuse to give up on who I am, and I refuse to abandon my destiny. I am one of a kind. I am a masterpiece. My identity is sure. I am comfortable in my own skin. My identity is loaded with gifts, talents, innate abilities, strengths, influence, affluence, and success. I embrace who I am, and who God has created and purposed me to be. Today and forever I am me. Beautifully and wonderfully made. With every new version of myself, I embrace, I love, I empower, and I inspire to be the very best of myself I can be. Me...born identity. I am fearfully and I am wonderfully made. I am a marvelous art of His works. My soul knows this right well.[56]

Chapter 4

Inexhaustible Power

"But ye shall receive power, after that the Holy Ghost is come upon you: and ye shall be witnesses unto me both in Jerusalem, and in all Judaea, and in Samaria, and unto the uttermost part of the earth." Acts 1:8[57]

We have been given power and authority to demonstrate the work of the Lord. So, when I say inexhaustible, I'm talking about we have THAT KIND OF "POWER" that NEVER GOES OUT. Every day we are loaded with power. The power that can move mountains. Power that can break shackles. The power that will cause us to walk right, talk right, and live right. The power that will make hell nervous. A power that will cause blinded eyes to see and deaf ears to hear. The power that mends broken relationships. How? Through the WORD we receive inexhaustible POWER released by the Holy Spirit.

When God marks us, He infuses us with POWER. I need you to get this. When He marks us, God gives us everything, whether we know it or not. It goes back to when he created us. He put everything that we would need in us. Over time we learned how to pull from this source of power, and we began to develop it, and eventually, we were able to use it.

But something different happens when we turn over our little power and connect with the Source Power. This only happens when we receive the Source (Jesus Christ) into our lives as Lord and Savior and receive the Holy Spirit. That's when we are able to walk in the demonstration of God's power on our lives.

> *"The Spirit of the Lord GOD is upon me; because the LORD hath anointed me to preach good tidings unto the meek; he hath sent me to bind up the brokenhearted, to proclaim liberty to the captives, and the opening of the prison to them that are bound; to proclaim the acceptable year of the LORD, and the day of vengeance of our God; to comfort all that mourn; to appoint unto them that mourn in Zion, to give unto them beauty for ashes, the oil of joy for mourning, the garment of praise for the spirit of heaviness; that they might be called trees of righteousness, the planting of the LORD, that he might be glorified."* Isaiah 61:1-3 (NKJV)[58]

> *"The Spirit of the Lord is upon me, because he hath anointed me to preach the gospel to the poor; he hath sent me to heal the brokenhearted, to preach deliverance to the captives, and recovering of sight to the blind, to set at liberty them that are bruised, to preach the acceptable year of the Lord."* Luke 4:18-19 (NKJV)[59]

You have something SPECIAL ON THE INSIDE OF YOU! Let me set the stage for you so you have a clear understanding of what you carry within you. For years I thought I was powerless. Nothing was changing for me. I was broken, confused, depressed, suicidal—hopeless.

I would try to step out to do things—I was very proactive, but somewhere down the pipeline everything I would resolve to do would come to a screeching halt. It felt like I had no say so in my thoughts or feelings. I felt helpless. Everyone would tell me how powerful I was, but I couldn't see it. I was WEAK. Weak in my faith, weak in studying the Word of God, weak as a wife, weak as a mother—just flat-out raggedy and weak. At least, that is what I was telling myself because those were my lived thoughts and realities.

However, I was only weak because I had not yet come into the true knowledge of who God called me to be and what He had called me to do. It's like walking around with car keys in your pocket and not understanding why the car won't start. Duh! The car can't start until you first take the keys out of your pocket, unlock the door, put the keys in the ignition, and turn the key.

I had the keys all along—I just didn't pull them out and use them. I was walking around with power, but I didn't know how to exercise my power. I thought I only had power when I was at church, but somehow when I left the church, the power it left too. I know I'm not the only person who has felt this way before. So, don't judge me.

I didn't believe that God found me worthy enough to be trusted with power on a regular basis. Do you see how sly the devil is? When you are not covered in faith and prayer, you'll get beat up by the lies of the devil so bad that you'll be tricked. Soooo...if you have found yourself in this sticky situation like mine. Let me tell you this. You are not a weakling. IT'S JUST TIME TO USE YOUR KEYS!

When we partner with the Holy Spirit, we'll be enabled to do all the things the scriptures tell us we can. He anoints us to do His works. We'll be able to lay hands on the sick and see them recover, preach deliverance to the captives and see them walk free, and heal the brokenhearted. We can only do this through the power of the Holy Spirit. You see, God permeates us with His exousia and dunamis power to get things done on earth through our spirits. So, what is exousia and dunamis?

Exousia (ex-oo-see'-ah) is a Greek word most often translated as "authority" or "power." We find in the Strong's Concordance -G1849 provides us with several descriptions that describe the exousia power. Exousia can be described as the "power of choice, the ability or strength with which one is endued, or a power which he either possesses or exercises (authority); a delegated influence: authority, jurisdiction, liberty, power, right, strength."[60] Yes. God has given us all of this. I learned that exousia power was originally given at Creation and was lost during the Fall of Man, but ultimately regained again through death and resurrection of Jesus Christ. Exousia power is not a feeling nor doesn't it require our feelings. However, it operates by a knowing (discernment) on the inside of us that causes our faith to align with our words, and then we are able to command and shape the spirit realm and the natural.

> *"For assuredly, I say to you, whoever says to this mountain, 'Be removed and be cast into the sea,' and does not doubt in his heart, but believes that those things he says will be done, he will have whatever he says."* Mark 11:23 (NKJV)[61]

Exousia power operates by the believer's faith. "Mountains move and are cast into the sea because I say so." Things must obey you. Exousia power is operating and exercising our God-given rights as children of God. This power causes both angels and demons to move at our word.

- Exousia has a higher rank than Dunamis. Exousia is what gives Dunamis. (Acts 8:19)
- Exousia is a spiritual authority that can be granted (or delegated). (Matt.10:1; Luke 4:6)
- Exousia has a sharpness that can either build or destroy. (2Cor.13:10)
- Exousia can also be abused by inappropriate use. (1Cor.9:18)

What in the world is Dunamis? In other translations, you may see it as *Dynamis*. Either way it's the explosive, miracle working, tangible power of God operating on the inside of us. According to the Strong's definition of dunamis *(doo'-nam-is)*; from G1410 is a "force (literally or figuratively); specially, miraculous power (usually by implication, a miracle itself):—

ability, abundance, meaning, might (-ily, -y, -y deed), (worker of) miracle(-s), power, strength, violence, mighty (wonderful) work."[62]

Dunamis is a tangible verified power. We see dunamis in full operation in the story of the woman of the issue of blood. *"and Jesus, immediately knowing in Himself that power had gone out of Him, turned around in the crowd and said, "Who touched My clothes?"* Mark 5:30 (NKJV) [63]

And also, with the woman with the spirit of infirmity. *"Now He was teaching in one of the synagogues on the Sabbath. And behold, there was a woman who had a spirit of infirmity eighteen years, and was bent over and could in no way [a]raise herself up. But when Jesus saw her, He called her to Him and said to her, "Woman, you are loosed from your infirmity." And He laid His hands on her, and immediately she was made straight, and glorified God."* Luke 13:10-13 (NKJV)[64]

Dunamis power is initiated by faith causing things to happen instantly. It is a result of producing action that causes things to shift and change immediately by enabling them to react swiftly both in the natural and spiritual realm. Dunamis power is also propelled by our compassion for others, so emotion can be involved. As with the woman with the spirit of infirmity, Jesus had compassion for her and wanted her to be whole.

The study of exousia and dunamis power is a great source for us and will have great impact on our lives. When we understand our true capabilities, we will refuse to lie down and die, but we will use what we have in our arsenals and command things to BREAK AWAY FROM US, IN US, AND AROUND US!

USE WHAT'S IN YOU. YOU ARE NOT A WEAKLING! YOU ARE A POWER PACKING, DEVIL STOMPING, MOUNTAIN MOVING, CHAIN BREAKING CHILD OF GOD!

We have to remember what God says concerning us. God has facilitated unto us power. Scriptures say, *"Now to Him who is able to do exceedingly abundantly above all that we ask or think, according to the power that works in us, to Him be glory in the church by Christ Jesus to all generations, forever and ever. Amen."* Ephesians 3:20-21 (NKJV)[65]

Think about that for a second. God is ABLE to do EXCEEDINGLY ABUNDANTLY...

Able- having the power, skill, means, or opportunity to do something; having considerable skill, proficiency, or intelligence.[66] Exceedingly- to an extreme degree. [67] Abundantly- marked by great plenty or amply supplied.[68] Our God in all of His intelligence—in all of His proficient power, skill, means, and opportunity to mark us by great plenty to an extreme degree according to the power that works in us. I can just jump, shout, and run on that! He marks us with great plenteous power to its extreme degree.

God in the greatness of His power—in its simplest form, is able to do what we ask?

The three definitions that describe God's ability shows us there is absolutely nothing that we could ask of God that supersedes His power to accomplish it. No matter what we inquire of Him no matter how common, great, or extensive the need maybe when know that He is able to go above that. When we ask for faith, forgiveness, the pardon of sin, salvation, healing, deliverance, favor, blessings, and undeserved grace and mercy; He goes above and beyond what was requested.

Now, think about all those times you asked God for these things. None of those things we could ask goes beyond God's POWER. I mean there is absolutely, positively—nothing we could ask that could. Consider what those in scripture ask of God. Yes, consider what the apostles, the prophets, the unbelievers, the heroes of faith asked from God; and look at what God did. God empowered them to do above what they could ever ask of Him! God exceeded the level of their expectation. What a mighty God we serve!

"Consider all that the children of God—past present and future have ever or will ever ask of Him and we will find nothing reaches beyond the scope of God's power." ~ George Mueller

God's power that works in us not long exceeds what we inquire of Him, but His power exceeds what we can think, imagine, or even dream of. There is absolutely nothing that we could think of that is beyond God's ability unless it contradicts His Word or Character such as sin.

So, the moment you think you have no power, and you ask God… Just know He'll supply you with more than enough. More than enough of ANYTHING. We are finite in power, but we are connected to a God who is infinite in POWER—INEXHAUSTIBLE POWER!

Scripture Walk—Kingdom Talk

In this section, we are going to walk through power scripture verses, because it is imperative to know what the word says about us. We need to know what we are carrying and the tools (words) found in our spiritual arsenals. This is a section you might want to bookmark because I'm going to provide you with a plethora of personalized scriptures that impress upon your external and internal growth and healing. Personalize? Yes. I'm going to structure them just for you so that you can declare them with confidence while making them your own. The Word of God has power. When we are marked by fire we must know how to handle the fire, because if not we just might burn ourselves. The Word of God not only gives power, but the Word also brings correction. We have to take it all. The Word of God does not discriminate, and the Word of God is not biased. The Word works for me just as it will work for you.

When you read and confess these verses you must say them and pray them out of faith while believing they are true. For instance, if someone you trust and who has proven themselves reliable, dependable, and trustworthy tells you that they are going to deposit $500 into your bank account—would you believe them? Absolutely you would! Why, because you trust their character. God's Word is just like that friend's word. God's Word is reliable, dependable, trustworthy, living, and it stands to defend itself. The Word of God has good character.

So, as you put your trust and faith in other things like sitting in a chair and believing it's going to hold your weight, or driving on the highway believing and trusting that people are going to stay in their lanes, or even flying on an airplane and trusting and believing the pilot will get you safely to your designation—we have to believe and trust the Word the same way. The Word of God is our POWER SOURCE. Are You Ready? LET DO THIS!

2 Corinthians 10:4 King James Version (KJV)
For the weapons of my warfare are not carnal, but mighty through God to the pulling down of strongholds.

2 Peter 1:3-4 New King James Version (NKJV)
God's divine power has given to me all things that pertain to life and godliness, through the knowledge of Him who called me by glory and virtue, by which have been given to me exceedingly great and precious promises, that through these I may be a partaker of the divine nature, having escaped the [a]corruption that is in the world through lust.

2 Timothy 1:7 New King James Version (NKJV)
For God has not given me a spirit of fear, but of power and of love and of a sound mind.

Isaiah 54:17 New King James Version (NKJV)
No weapon formed against me shall prosper, and every tongue which

rises against me in judgment I shall condemn.

Psalm 18:35 New King James Version (NKJV)
You have also given me the shield of Your salvation, and Your right hand upholds me; and Your gentleness makes me great.

Psalm 118:6 New King James Version (NKJV)
The Lord is on my side; I will not fear. What can man do to me?

1 Corinthians 15:57 New King James Version (NKJV)
Thanks be to God, who gives me the victory through our Lord Jesus Christ.

Deuteronomy 20:4 New King James Version (NKJV)
The Lord my God is He who goes with me, to fight for me against my enemies, to save me.'

Ephesians 6:12 King James Version (KJV)
For I do not wrestle against flesh and blood, but against principalities, against powers, against the rulers of the darkness of this world, against spiritual wickedness in high places.

1 Corinthians 15:58 New King James Version (NKJV)
I am steadfast, immovable, always abounding in the work of the Lord, knowing that my labor is not in vain in the Lord.

Acts 1:8 New King James Version (NKJV)
I have power because the Holy Spirit has come upon me; and I shall be a witnesses of Jesus unto the uttermost parts of the earth.

Ephesians 6:10 New King James Version (NKJV)
I will be strong in the Lord and in the strength of His might.

Luke 10:19 New King James Version (NKJV)
I have been given the authority to trample on serpents and scorpions, and over all the power of the enemy, and nothing shall by any means hurt me.

Philippians 4:13 New King James Version (NKJV)
I can do all things through Christ which strengthens me.

Colossians 1:13 New King James Version (KJV)
He has delivered me from the power of darkness and translated me into the kingdom of His dear Son,

2 Corinthians 12:9 New King James Version (NKJV)
God's grace is sufficient for me, and His strength is made perfect in my weakness." Therefore most gladly I will rather boast in my infirmities, that the power of Christ may rest upon me.

Ephesians 3:20 New King James Version (NKJV)
Now to Him who is able to do exceedingly abundantly above all that I ask or think, according to the power that works in me.

1 Peter 2:9 New King James Version (NKJV)
I am a chosen generation, a royal priesthood, a holy nation, I am His own special possession, that I may proclaim the praises of Him who called me out of darkness into His marvelous light.

Ephesians 4:22-23 New King James Version (NKJV)
I put off all things concerning my former conduct, the old man which grows corrupt according to the deceitful lusts, and I am renewed in the spirit of your mind, and I will put on the new man which was created according to God, in true righteousness and holiness.

Romans 12:2 New King James Version (NKJV)
I will not be conformed to this world, but I will be transformed by the renewing of my mind, so that I may prove what is that good and acceptable and perfect will of God.

2 Corinthians 5:17 New King James Version (NKJV)
I am in Christ, so I am a new creation; old things have passed away; behold, all things have become new.

Psalm 139:14 New King James Version (NKJV)
I will praise You, for I am fearfully and wonderfully made; marvelous are Your works, and that my soul knows very well.

Philippians 4:13 New King James Version (NKJV)
I can do all things through Christ who strengthens me.

Isaiah 41:10 New King James Version (NKJV)
I will fear not, for God is with me; I will not be dismayed, for He is my God. God will strengthen Me, Yes, God will help me, He will uphold me with His righteous right hand.'

Deuteronomy 31:6 New King James Version (NKJV)
I am strong and of good courage, I will not fear nor will I be afraid; for the Lord my God, He is the One who goes with me. He will not leave me nor forsake me.

Isaiah 40:31 New King James Version (NKJV)
I will wait on the Lord and He shall renew my strength; I will mount up with wings like eagles; I will run and not be weary; and I will walk and not faint.

Exodus 15:2 New King James Version (NKJV)
The Lord is my strength and my song, and He is my salvation; He is my God, and I will praise Him, and I will exalt him.

1 Corinthians 10:13 New King James Version (NKJV)
There is no temptation that will overtake me that is not common to man. God is faithful, and He will not let me be tempted beyond my ability, but with every temptation He will also provide the way of escape, that I may be able to endure it.

Deuteronomy 20:4 New King James Version (NKJV)
For the Lord my God is He who goes with me to fight against my enemies and gives me victory.

2 Corinthians 12:9-10 New King James Version (NKJV)
God's grace is sufficient for me, His power is made perfect in my weakness. Therefore, I will boast all the more gladly of my weaknesses, so that the power of Christ may rest upon me. For the sake of Christ, I am content with weaknesses, insults, hardships, persecutions, and calamities. For when I am weak, then God is made strong.

Joshua 1:9 New King James Version (NKJV)
I will be strong and courageous. I will not be frightened, and I will not be dismayed, for the Lord my God is with me wherever you go.

Philippians 4:8 New King James Version (NKJV)
I will think on things that are true, things that are noble, things that are just, things that are pure, things that lovely, things that are of good report, and on I will think on anything that is of virtue and anything praiseworthy—I will meditate on these things.

Isaiah 12:2 New King James Version (NKJV)
God is my salvation; I will trust Him and I will not be afraid. For the Lord God is my strength and my song, and He is my salvation.

Matthew 11:28 New King James Version (NKJV)
I will come to the Lord and lay down all of my labor and my heaviness, and He will give me rest.

Isaiah 40:29 New King James Version (NKJV)
God gives power to me when I am weak in strength, and He increases strength.

Psalm 27:1-3 New King James Version (NKJV)
The Lord is my light and my salvation; whom shall I fear? The Lord is the stronghold of my life; of whom shall I be afraid? When the wick comes against me to eat up my flesh, my enemies and foes, will stumble and fell. Even when an army encamps against me, my heart shall not fear; even though war may rise against me, in this I will be confident.

Psalm 73:26 New King James Version (NKJV)
My flesh and my heart may fail, but God is the strength of my heart and my portion forever.

Mark 12:30 New King James Version (NKJV)
I will love the Lord my God with all my heart and with all my soul and with all my mind and with all my strength.

Psalm 46:1^b New King James Version (NKJV)
God is my refuge and strength, a very present help in trouble.

Psalm 18:32-34 New King James Version (NKJV)
It is God who arms me with strength, and makes my way perfect. He

makes my feet like the feet of deer, and sets me on my high places. He teaches my hands to make war, So that my arms can bend a bow of bronze.

John 16:33[b] New King James Version (NKJV)
In the world I will have tribulation, but I will take heart, because Jesus have already overcome the world.

Matthew 6:33 New King James Version (NKJV)
I will seek first the kingdom of God and His righteousness, and all these things will be added to me.

Psalm 23:4 New King James Version (NKJV)
Even though I walk through the valley of the shadow of death, I will fear no evil, for God is with me; His rod and His staff, will comfort me.

2 Thessalonians 3:3 New King James Version (NKJV)
The Lord is faithful. He will establish me and guard me against the evil one.

Romans 8:37 New King James Version (NKJV)
Yet in all these things I am more than conquerors through Jesus Christ who loved us.

1 John 4:4 New King James Version (NKJV)
God who is in me is greater than he who is in the world.

Jeremiah 29:11-14[a] New King James Version (NKJV)
For God knows the thoughts that He think toward me, thoughts of peace and not of evil, to give me a future and a hope. I will call upon the on Him and I will, and God will listen to me, and when I seek Him and I will find Him. When I search for Him with all my heart He will be found, and the Lord will bring me out of bondage.

Philippians 4:6-7 New King James Version (NKJV)
I will be anxious for nothing, but in everything by prayer and supplication, with thanksgiving, I will make my requests made known to God; and the peace of God, which surpasses all understanding, will guard my heart and mind through Christ Jesus

2 Corinthians 4:7 New King James Version (NKJV)
I have this treasure in this earthen vessel that the excellence of the power may be of God and not of myself.

I pray that these scriptures will push you over the edge into a greater dimension of faith. When you hide the Word of God in your heart, you will exude inexhaustible POWER. Use what you have and don't allow the enemy to run all over you. The Word of God reminds us of who we are. Yes. It reminds that us that WE ARE POWERFUL BEINGS! When we are made aware of the power of the Word given to us, we are DANGEROUS and pose a threat to the kingdom of darkness! So, use your key of VICTORY because there is inexhaustible power in the Word of God.

Come Out of Lo Debar

For us to operate in inexhaustible power; we have to see ourselves correctly. How we perceive ourselves determines the way we respond to things that come against us or even things that happen to us—no matter how good or bad. I'm going to give a biblical example of this. Let's take a look at our friend Mephibosheth.

Mephibosheth was the son of Jonathan, grandson of King Saul, and father of Mica or Micha. His mother is never mentioned in his upbringing, but after researching I found that her name was Rizpah, and she was one of Saul's concubines.

Mephibosheth was five years old when both his father and grandfather died at the Battle of Mount Gilboa. According to the biblical narrative when he was under the care of a nurse when she received word that his father, Jonathan, and grandfather, Saul were killed. In her haste, the nurse dropped him, and due to the fall, he ended up permanently crippled in both feet. Read 2 Samuel 4:4

You see back during those days if you were disabled or

diseased you were frowned upon and placed in a category of impossibilities and incapability. How many times have you ever felt crippled after a fall? A fall that ultimately shifted your perspective of life in its entirety. I know I have experienced this...

You may not have been physically crippled, but life may have hurled you things that caused you to become crippled in your thinking, crippled in your emotions, crippled in your mind, and crippled in your belief system. You can't see past what has happened to you—so you run—and you hide. You hide behind your gifts, your abilities, your wit, your logic, your personality, and your beautiful smile. You want to avoid the realization that you've been dropped—pretending that the fall never caused you any damage.

You see, when the nurse fled with Mephibosheth, he had no choice but to go where she was taking him. Some of us have also been taken into places beyond our control. We found ourselves in a tight, lonely, angry, remorseful spot. We don't even know why it happened—we just know that it happened to leave us with scarred evidence. Those scars caused us to dwell, hide, and adjust to a low place. (Lo-debar)

Metaphysical meaning of Lo-Debar

Lo-Debar, (Hebrew)-without order; disorderly; no leader; not governed; rebellious; no shepherd; without pasture; no issue; barren; without speech; dumb; not the word or oracle; false; untrue. [69] Meta- the disorderly, undisciplined, barren, substance-less (without pasture), and un-illumined, a state into which the consciousness of man comes when the personal will (Saul) has been exercised without restraint.[70]

Lo-debar was a place. A place that represented people who were considered insignificant. Lo Debar would house the lost, unskilled, and uneducated outcasts from society. Those whom people would scorn, those who were passed by in the streets with no regard. Sadly, some of us are in Lo-debar, have been in Lo-debar for quite some time.

You see, Mephibosheth was not in Lo Debar because of something he had done. Yet, he spent his days being cared for by someone else all while living under the rules and opinions others. He had to live off handouts from others in a forgotten place called "Lo Debar". What I love about this story is that even in our low places God's love tracks us down and calls us out.

We see in the book of 2 Samuel 9 David sought out to show kindness to the house of Saul on behalf of his friend Jonathan. David called out Mephibosheth from the place of Lo-debar. When God marks us, He sends word for us. Even if the people around us don't feel as though we're up to par.

Now David said, "Is there still anyone who is left of the house of Saul, that I may show him [a]kindness for Jonathan's sake?" And there was a servant of the house of Saul whose name was Ziba. So when they had called him to David, the king said to him, "Are you Ziba?" He said, "At your service." Then the king said, "Is there not still someone of the house of Saul, to whom I may show the kindness of God?" And Ziba said to the king, "There is still a son of Jonathan who is lame in his feet." So the king said to him, "Where is he?" And Ziba said to the king, "Indeed he is in the house of Machir the son of Ammiel, in Lo Debar." 2 Samuel 9:1-5[71]

David said to Ziba, "I want to show kindness to the house of Saul." Right? So, why was Ziba's response to bring up the condition of Mephibosheth? Why did he have to bring up Mephibosheth's lame feet? I'm sure Ziba was thinking, 'why in the world are you asking about him? Mephibosheth is marked in such a way that I don't think his name should even be on the king's tongue, nor should he be seeking him out. He is in LO-DEBAR, for crying out loud.' Sadly, our conditions are more recognizable than the call on our lives.

People will immediately categorize others by their condition and not by their purpose. They may never know or understand why God allowed us to through such struggle or testing. They will never understand the pressing, the breaking, and the stripping. I'm not saying every time God wants to mark an individual, He places them through struggle. What I'm saying is, sometimes struggle helps the onlookers to recognize that God is behind the struggle and is faithful and powerful enough to bring them out. Mephibosheth, nor did we decide to go to Lo-debar on our own free will.

We see in the following verses that when Mephibosheth came to David afraid. Even though he knew he did no wrong. Not only did he have a physical condition, but Lo-debar conditioned his mind in such a way that when the king requested his presence—something within him thought that something had to be wrong. JESUS! Low places will condition us to be afraid of the king's request, because as I pointed out, Lo-debar was a place that represented people who were considered insignificant. The mindset of those of Lo-debar had been shaped by their conditions and their environment. So, it would cause a person to question the request of destiny.

> *Now when Mephibosheth[b] the son of Jonathan, the son of Saul, had come to David, he fell on his face and prostrated himself. Then David said, "Mephibosheth?" And he answered, "Here is your servant." So David said to him, "Do not fear, for I will surely show you kindness for Jonathan your father's sake, and will restore to you all the land of Saul your grandfather; and you shall eat bread at my table continually." Then he bowed himself, and said, "What is your servant, that you should look upon such a dead dog as I?"* 2 Samuel 9:6-8 [72]

Lo-debar Provides Perspective

Can you imagine how Mephibosheth felt after all those years of being forced to live in a condition that was not of his own doing? How might those years shape his thoughts, sights, and perspectives of life and himself? When he came before the king, he was hopeless and felt powerless. Fear strips us of power. His response to the king was fear, and then he criticized himself. His condition caused him to think lowly of his own being.

What lenses or scope do you look through when you look at your life, your relationships, your career path, your money, your time, your talent, your spirituality, or your purpose? What has conditioned you to see life in that way? If your condition has made you want to refuse the request of the king, then it's time to shift gears to find the root so that it may be uprooted. When we are in Christ, our old condition is no longer a part of who we are. We are liberated to sever the ties to the old man. *"Therefore, if anyone is in Christ, he is a new creation; old things have passed away; behold, all things have become new."* 2 Corinthians 5:17 (NKJV)[73]

Perspective can be described as "a mental view or prospect; one giving a distinctive impression of distance; the capacity to view things in their true relations or relative importance. Perspective gives us the capacity to view things in their true relevance and importance.

Think about that. If we believe a lie as being our truth—that lie will shape everything else around us and will operate and function in accordance.

How we perceive ourselves will determine the amount of power we feel we have. Why? Because if we see ourselves small, broken, weak, and inadequate, we begin to feel powerless. Say this out loud, "I AM SHIFTING MY PERSPECTIVE"!

So...what happen with Mephibosheth?

And the king called to Ziba, Saul's servant, and said to him, "I have given to your master's son all that belonged to Saul and to all his house. You therefore, and your sons and your servants, shall work the land for him, and you shall bring in the harvest, that your master's son may have food to eat. But Mephibosheth your master's son shall eat bread at my table always." Now Ziba had fifteen sons and twenty servants. Then Ziba said to the king, "According to all that my lord the king has commanded his servant, so will your servant do." "As for Mephibosheth," said the king, "he shall eat at my table like one of the king's sons." Mephibosheth had a young son whose name was Micha. And all who dwelt in the house of Ziba were servants of Mephibosheth. So Mephibosheth dwelt in Jerusalem, for he ate continually at the king's table. And he was lame in both his feet. 2 Samuel 9:9-13 (NKJV)[74]

The kindness of the king shifted Mephibosheth's life forever. He was considered a son of the king! Even those who could only associate him with his condition had to now recognize him as royalty. And not only him but his lineage (his son). God's grace calls us out of Lo-debar, and changes our status, and allows us to dwell at His table forever.

It wasn't Mephibosheth's fault his father died, and it wasn't his fault the nurse dropped him. It wasn't his fault that no doctor could repair his situation. You see, it wasn't your fault that you were molested; it wasn't your fault that you were abused-verbally or physically; it is not your fault you had no father, no mother; it is not your fault that you had to raise yourself, your siblings, and maybe your parents too—instead of them raising you. It's not your fault that you see yourself as nothing, as nobody, or unworthy of being a blessing or of substance. No matter how you may word it, please understand that you are not what happened to you. That *drop* does not determine your value; nor does it determine the power that God has released to you. Come out of Lo-debar. You're carrying something great. You have something special on the inside of you, and you've been chosen to sit at the king's table to eat.

How You See Yourself Determines Your Power

If we are going to walk in the inexhaustible power of God,

we must see ourselves correctly. For years I saw this distorted version of myself. That picture drove my thoughts, my behaviors, and even the people I attracted. How we see ourselves will establish this false value of worth. It's like putting a three dollar price tag on a twelve-carat diamond when the value of that diamond is worth so much more. This is often what we do to ourselves. God marked us with extreme value and purchased us at an extreme cost—yet we reduced that value and cost to mere pennies. So how can we begin to see ourselves through the eyes of God?

You must first target the deceitful thoughts and voices inside your heads. Paying close attention to the thoughts you allow to circulate in your mind. You must do three things: investigate, evaluate, and eliminate.

Investigate your thoughts

Let's look at the definition of investigate. Investigate- to search out and examine the particulars of in an attempt to learn the facts about something hidden, unique, or complex, especially in an attempt to find a motive, cause, or culprit. [75]

We are charged with bringing our thoughts captive and bringing them under the subjection of Christ. We are to judge our thoughts. So, as thoughts come across our minds, how we process them is important. We have to ask ourselves, *"Where is the origin of this thought? Is this thought true or false? Does it align with who God says that I am?"*

It is not okay to allow idle thoughts to swirl through our heads. Healthy thoughts allow us to operate with greater power. You are what you think. The enemy will feed you lies and deception, and if you began to eat them then you'll become them. However, all the enemy can do is suggest things to you. It's up to you to determine what you are going to eat and digest. The scripture puts this plainly for us. *"For as he thinks in his heart, so is he. "Eat and drink." he says to you, but his heart is not with you."* Proverbs 23:7 (NKJV)[76]

The devil will give us poisoned food and drink knowing it will kill us. His lies are subtle and convincing. He even transforms himself as an angel of light.[77] So, investigating our thoughts are as important as our next breath. If he can get us to believe in what we're thinking, then he can foil and frustrate our purpose. Our purpose is the reason we live. Next, we must evaluate.

Evaluate Your Thoughts

Evaluate- to determine or set the value or amount of; appraise: to evaluate property; to judge or determine the significance, worth, or quality of; assess.[78]

We are to determine the set value of our thoughts. We must appraise them, judge them, and determine their significance, worth, or quality. My God from heaven, that's good information! When thoughts cross our minds, we must evaluate their value. We have to judge to see if there is any significance to the thoughts.

This makes me think of the scripture found in Philippians 4: 8-9 where we are instructed to think on the things that are true, noble, just, pure, lovely, of good report, of virtue, and praiseworthy.

When we are bombarded with thoughts, we must judge them. If we don't, those thoughts will begin to shape our perception, our imagination, and our belief system; and eventually strip us of our faith and identity found in Christ. Why because, false thinking diminishes the truth, and it's the truth that makes us free in Christ Jesus.[79] Lastly, we must eliminate.

Eliminate Your Thoughts

After we investigate and evaluate, we must eliminate. To eliminate means to omit, especially as being unimportant or irrelevant; leave out: to eradicate or kill.[80] We are to omit, eradicate, or kill all unimportant and irrelevant thoughts. Negative thoughts and poor thinking—hinder, stifle, debilitate, and halt our progress, growth, and development. If you want to live a life of inexhaustible power then you must watch guard your thoughts and discard those that serve no purpose. I'm sure you heard of that phrase "The mind is a terrible thing to waste." It's very true. Guard your mind at all cost because eventually, you will begin to speak your thoughts.

Watch Your Words

I can write so much about this topic. What we allow to come out of our mouths is just as important as the thoughts we allow to reside in our minds. Just like thoughts can shape our perceptions; words also have the power to shape our world. Mahatma Gandhi says, *"Watch your thoughts. For they become words. Watch your words. For they become actions. Watch your actions. For they become habits. Watch your Habits. For they become character. Watch your character. For it becomes your destiny."*

Eventually, our thoughts will leave our heads and come out of our mouths. When we speak, we create. When we assign a name to something, we give it an identity. Remember? Words are what God used to create the world. The spoken word of God was a force that framed and brought forth the world into existence—a word spoken did this. Words have creative power. Without words the world would not have been formed, nor would there be the existence of life- no humans, animals, plants, or trees, etc. It was with a few words that God created light. "Let there be." With God forming us into His image and after His likeness…we have that same creative power. So, we have to be careful. The next time you want to speak something—make sure it's something worth creating.

The words of our mouths are fruit. We reap what we sow into them, this includes both good and bad produce. For instance. I have some family members and friends that use the term *broke* to describe when they're low on funds. The term broke has a multitude of meanings. That confession is not only limited to their money. That confession now can take residence in any area of their lives. They identified that they were broke in their funds, but now we see that word causing them to be broke in their emotions, broke in their creativity, broke in their influence, broke in their confidence, broke in the behaviors, and other areas where they can be broken. We are to enjoy the fruit of our words.

When God spoke and created it brought Him satisfaction. He would create and say, "It was good" and with man it was very good". What can you say about your creation? *"A man will be satisfied with good by the fruit of his mouth, and the recompense of a man's hands will be rendered to him."* Proverbs 12:14 (NKJV)

Say what you want, not what you have. You have creative power in your tongue. What we think and speak determines our power source. I will close out this chapter with another affirmation. I am a big believer in affirmations. I believe the more you say it; the more you will see it manifest in the natural. If you have a moment and need a reminder of how powerful you are, just turn to this chapter to remind yourself of the inexhaustible power within you.

(SPEAK IT OUT LOUD)

You can have what you speak, and you can become what you think.

AFFIRMATION: I am Powerful

I am powerful. I am strong mentally, emotionally, spiritually, and physically. I excel in power. I can leap over a wall and run through a troop. I'm powerful enough to complete every God-ordained assignment on my life. I am sober-minded, conscious, and vigilant. I am not weak. I am not beggarly. I am efficient. I am adequate. I have what it takes to do what God has purposed me to do. I operate and run off of all cylinders. God is my partner, and through Him, I live, and I move, and I have my being. We are one. With God, I'm unstoppable. I'm unbeatable. I can do all things; exceedingly, abundantly, and above all, I can ask or think.

Power is working on this inside of me. I can speak a thing, and it will be established. I can speak a thing, and it will be manifested. I have mountain-moving power. I have purpose producing power. I have influential power. I'm blessed. The power that I have supersedes me. It goes before me and dispels all darkness. I'm drenched and undergirded by the power of God. I can't be stopped. I refuse to be intimidated. I refuse to allow my purpose to be snuffed out or watered down.

I embrace my God-given power. I allow it to kindle on the inside of me. The Spirit of the Lord is at work in me, and I am who He says that I am, and I AM POWERFUL!

PART III
MARKED FOR HISTORY

Chapter 5

Born To Start Fires

"For this very purpose I have raised you up, that I may show My power in you, and that My name may be declared in all the earth." Romans 9:17$_a$ (NKJV)[81]

This is the chapter of grace and empowerment. I am so excited about this chapter because I will be able to fan your flames by reminding you of who God says that you are. I will be on my soapbox but in a good way. Up to this point, I was establishing a foundation to push you in your proper place as a Firestarter. Throughout these pages, I shared pieces of myself with you. I shared my insecurities, my struggles, my shortcomings, my pain, my insight, and my beliefs and thoughts. Now I'm going to share my FIRE.

The first association with the term fire came when I was asked to minister in dance in the summer of 2010. As I entered into the sanctuary clothed in my dance garments taking my place at the front of the church, the moderator of the service shouted out, "my God, I feel the fire of God." Focused on the assignment at hand, I didn't take into consideration of what God was saying through the woman of God or even aware of what was happening or what happened in that moment. However, that statement began to resonate in my heart and spirit the entire night. I left the service, and that statement continued to roll over in my spirit. God took that moment to bring awareness to something that I supernaturally carried and operated in and under.

Years passed, but I kept that statement near to my heart. When asked to minister in dance, that woman's face and voice was all I could see, and I could hear. "I can feel the fire of God". My thoughts couldn't comprehend it. What does the fire of God feel like? I had not yet experienced the fire of God in this way before, but yet this woman made this announcement as I walked by her to get in to place.

On the inside of me, I wanted others to feel that same way. I knew that only God could bring about that feeling, but I didn't know how to initiate it or engage it—so like in the previous chapters you saw how I would just blow things off. I did the same with this statement as well and simply wrote it off as a one-time instance.

Over time, I began to increase my prayer times, I started to learn more, receive more, and do more. I started to receive prophecy after prophecy regarding the fire of God, but I didn't take heed. Not because I was rebellious—it was just that I didn't believe it. I started to allow my personal opinions and the opinions of others to outweigh the voice of God and allowed others to dictate what God place down on the inside of me. I didn't feel worthy enough to carry such a gift. I'm so glad we have a God that doesn't care about what others or even what we think about what He places down on the inside of us. He wants to manifest through us what He wills into the earth. Opinions don't matter to Him. After all, He is the God of creation! The only opinion that matters is HIS.

Year after year, God's voice continued to become more prominent in conjunction with myself and fire. I continued with life constantly battling with the woman I was—with the woman I so desperately wanted to become. I wanted to be confident, strong, needed, chosen, accepted, and influential—a woman of FIRE. Even though I possessed all of those qualities, my belief systems fought against it. I was so frustrated. I judged myself so harshly, and little by little my flame had dwindled.

It was 2014, and we were in the full swing of prepping for The Awakening Women's Encounter. I held the registration coordinator's role for about four years during this time. This conference was one of our biggest women's encounters we would host each year. While prepping, I would always become overwhelmed because I wanted everything perfect, but I always felt that I seemed to fall short of reaching that level of expectation. This event became personal to me, as I would throw so much of myself into it to make sure everything and everyone was happy, comfortable, and catered to from the little role I played. I was sincere in everything I would do, but every year it seemed like I would find myself in a rut days leading up to the event. What in the world was this? I couldn't pinpoint it, but I knew I wanted it to stop. Why was this happening?

On the first day of the conference, everything was going well until everyone received these extravagant personal prophetic words from the Lord, and I received nothing. However, a Word came that God was going to replace the administrator, not because they were bad, but because the church needed someone with skills in advanced technology. Grief overtook me, I was being replaced, and I did not receive a personal prophetic word. Total boomer! Plus, all that week I cried out to the Lord asking if He could please just speak to me, but I didn't know that God wanted me fired and didn't want to speak to me (Lack of spiritual maturity). When I didn't get a word that night, I instantly thought that God didn't care about me, because of all the wrong I had done in my life (Rejection). Immediately, the thoughts came rushing in like a heard of wild buffalo; one after the other. I couldn't sleep that night as I was so grieved in spirit. I tried my best to shake it off because the next day I had to put on a good face.

The following morning, I was weighed down like a ton of bricks. I kept telling myself to pull it together. The stress, coupled with anxiety, upset my stomach. I made a phone call so I could go home and get myself together. I tried to rationalize my emotions and thoughts, but I was stuck. I felt so embarrassed. There I was, 30 years old and pouting about not receiving a prophetic word. What in the whole tribe of Judah was going on with me?!

I finally arrived at church, and all the women and staff were happy and chipper, yet there I was trying to push through. My pastor pulled me and another sister aside to share her breakthrough. I was genuinely excited for her, and also for the other sister, but their breakthrough reminded me of my ignored request all over again. What I was going through had absolutely nothing to do with them, but everything to do with the chains of the demonic spirits of rejection, orphan, and deception choking me out. I needed help. As the day went on, the pressure intensified. I went to my car numerous of times and just wept. "Lord, please just help me, PLEASE." I also called one of my friends who stayed in Texas to pray for me. I was hurting, and I felt powerless.

I tried to pull myself together in the best way possible, no one even recognized I was gone, so I continued with my tasks as well as I could, trying to avoid every person I felt could see right through my painted smile. I just needed to get through this day. **Note I was a big avoider and isolator back then** Two of the nastiest spirits that will eat you alive if you don't receive deliverance from them.

As we were nearing our last service, a woman of God preached a powerful and comforting Word. It was much needed and befitting for me. What I recalled from the message was God was still able to speak to us and use us even in our poor condition, because He was the One who was able to heal and deliver us. We just had to be willing to give Him a "Yes", even when things hurt, didn't feel good, or didn't work in our desired favor. I started to feel a bit lighter after hearing her testimony and listening to the Word. The opportunity for an altar call was offered, and she called up her team. I knew I needed to get to her. Maybe she could help with my much-needed breakthrough. WRONG, WRONG, WRONG! God had other plans, as her team started forming the lines, and I ended up in a line that led to a young man who I knew of from a previous event. I knew he was anointed, but my heart was set on the Pastor Karen.

As I walked up to him, he uttered, "I feel the fire of God." He had my attention! A Word so candid and so familiar. As I made my way closer, he declared, "Woman of God, You carry the fire of God in your belly, and you will preach the word of God radically and with fire." I wept before God. Like, what did this mean? I was trying to understand how God could use such a person who was such a broken mess. I spent most of that day bound up, yet I was praying that others would get free. What was wrong with me? Now, I just received the Word that I'm carrying the fire of God, and I'm supposed to preach with fire? Something has to be off. God couldn't possibly want to use me to preach His Word...could He?

I never told a soul of that Word because I thought they would surely laugh right in my face. But the Holy Spirit ascribed that Word on the tablet of my heart and wouldn't let me forget it. I fought so hard against that Word. I tried my best to disqualify myself from it. Now, you can see the mess God was working on fixing. I was a hot raggedy mess. Jesus take the wheel!

Time went on, but I still found myself struggling with emotional triggers without rhyme or reason. There was no untouched area of my life that was not affected by these triggers. There would be days when I would just wake up in a rut. It was madness. I pushed through day by day. Some days were better than others.

The close of the year was approaching, and I had written down some things I wanted to work on in the New Year. When we finally brought in 2015, things were going to be better. The theme for this year was to write the vision. I took that theme seriously, as I etched it onto my vision board, but it still felt like I was moving backward instead of forward.

I continued pressing forward, but to no avail, as nothing could penetrate the loneliness and heaviness I felt. I was depressed…real depressed. The depression I started to experience stemmed from several things. I was over-extending myself, and I wanted to be there for others although my own life was tumultuous. My marriage was on the rocks, my children were going through some things, my husband and I were experiencing financial struggles; and this all led to frustration because no one seemed to be noticing my needs. I felt like I needed someone in my corner during this time, and yet I was still too busy trying to do for others while forsaking myself. I was sinking, and it seemed like I was invisible to everyone around me. The only thing that mattered was "them, their stuff, what they had going on, or what/how they felt." My frustration turned to anger—which turned into rage.

How was it that I able to show up for others during their time of need, but there I was fighting all alone. Those feelings led me to the transitioning and demotion of position from Church Administrator and Pastor's assistant. The decision cut through me like a knife. However, I understood that this decision wasn't personal, and necessary for the ministry, but during that time it sure felt like it was.

The voice in my head confirmed every feeling thrown at my heart. *"Patrea, I told you that you'd never be loved, needed, or wanted. You will never be smart enough, good enough, or capable of doing what God says. You gave it your all, now you should give up.*

God does not need you, and these people don't need or want you. All they are going to do is use you. You don't matter! You tried this church stuff long enough, now it's time to give it up."

I cried for months and months. I really wanted to be better, but I just couldn't breakthrough. I tried my hardest, but my hardest wasn't good enough. I fought to stay happy. I fought to stay above water, but I was drowning fast. Once the transition took place, my phone stopped ringing, some people stopped calling me, and others even stopped speaking to me. It was devastating. The transition of the role was so I could get the nurturing that I needed, but by this time I was broken.

I couldn't take any more hurt. I was broken, fragmented, and torn. I became as hard as a rock on my exterior. I did my best while serving on the dance and praise team, but the guilt, anger, disappointment, and shame started to take a toll on me. How could I sing about a God and His faithfulness, but yet be so angry with Him? How could I dance about a God that would allow me to suffer this kind of hurt all alone while others could go on with living life even after hurting me—not being there for me? How could He cause my heart to be so big and generous towards them—people in general, but allow others to be so closed hurt to me sore? Then act as if everything was my fault! It was so unfair. I dealt with their rough moments. I was there for their uncertain moments. I dealt with their lashing out, and I dealt with their other stuff too. So, why was my stuff so bad or so difficult for others to handle?

How could they get a pass, and their wrongs be overlooked, and my wrongs caused me to be ostracized? I couldn't understand it for the life of me. I didn't know why it was okay for others to keep a record of what they'd done for me, as though I never did anything or added any value to them. I finally asked if I could just take a season off from singing and dancing. I needed my heart to be right. I needed God to heal what was broken in me. During this time, I tried to show up in my marriage and mothering the best way I possibly could. I never stopped attending church or church functions. It was hard for me at times, but my commitment to God would not let me quit. I believe it was God's hand on me because it was surely painful losing relationships and losing invites to events and functions. Yet, I still continued to do my best and show up; and not just in church, but in who I was. People went on, and I remained stuck in the pain.

Months crawled by for me. I was not working, and I stayed home sinking. No one called or stopped by to check in on me. My marriage was in critical condition, and my children were suffering. Occasionally, I would get a phone call or two. I would play melancholy. I refused to let anyone in my world at this point. My thoughts would be, "why are you calling now? I didn't need any sympathy, and I didn't need anyone keeping a record of how many times they called to check in on me." As life would have it…everyone went on living their best life, and I was trapped—dying.

It got to the point where I almost wanted to vomit when I would hear the phrase "If one of us is hurting—we are all hurting." I despised that saying because I was not only hurting. I was hurting and broken. It wasn't fair that everyone who came around seemed to be doing fine. Again, some did profess their thoughts of me or stated I was on their mind, but they forgot to call. This made me feel worse.   Where were the discerning people of God? I was suicidal and wanted to kill myself and no one had a clue. Jesus help us all!

Time continued to pass, and I continued to keep to myself. I was implementing different strategies to break into something new. I went to counseling, I tried to be more positive, and I started praying again. I tried everything to make the pain and emptiness go away. I still maintained my attendance in church and other events. Church was all I knew to do since I was a little girl, and since I made that commitment to God at 18 years old. I knew nothing outside of churching.

The Awakening Women's Encounter had touched the lives of so many women that the team continued with doing both The Awakening Women's Encounter and the newest faculty The Awakening Reload were in works simultaneously. During our second Awakening Reloaded event, I sat in my seat numb, as I watched all the smiling faces pass me by, occasionally I would share a hug and smooch on the cheek with some of the ladies. I was there to support. I didn't have any expectation for God to do anything for me. I had ultimately given up at this point. The low place consumed me. I was broken, angry, resentful, prayerless, and full of myself. I couldn't shake myself free.

The hurt, the shame, and the disappointment paralyzed me. I was in the atmosphere of healing and deliverance, but nothing could permeate the thick walls I built. I was numb—pretending to be okay—yet empty. The service had come to an end, and I gathered my things and started heading for the door. My pastor stopped me and asked if anyone had prayed for me? I shook my head and told her that it was okay. She (Pastor Kimberly) then waved her hand, and the Awakening Team: Pastor Toemeika, Pastor Nedra, Elder Mamie, Prophetess Carla, and Elder Shonda swooped me up, and a few of ladies prayed for me audibly, as the others prayed and agreed silently.

It is important to note that each woman walked powerfully in their individual calling and anointing, however, on this day...Prophetess Carla stood before me. Let me put a staple right here to explain. So, the way God operates through Prophetess Carla is oftentimes radical, sometimes unusual, but all the time powerful. She prophesies with boldness and with accuracy. She is the "real deal" when it comes to the things of God. Especially, when it comes to the prophetic ministry.

So, I'm standing there surrounded. I couldn't run even if I wanted to. At that moment, my fate was sealed. Prophetess

Carla began to pray. Then she began to call out things that were hindering my breakthrough. I began to weep before God. Then she shifted gears and began to prophesy. *"Patrea you carry the fire of God, but you have to forgive. You are persecuting with no cause."*, but I wasn't exactly sure of what that meant. I'm carrying the fire of God, but I had to forgive...and I'm persecuting with no cause? I was floored. If I were to persecute someone there was definitely a reason. As a matter of fact, I wasn't even talking to people at this point, and I surely wasn't gossiping about the people who hurt me. No, I didn't *have* to forgive them, I thought to myself. Those people chose to hurt me.

As I look back, I realize that God was reaffirming his faith in me. God sent a Word to remind me of what He had spoken to me years prior in 2010. My feelings and poor perception of myself overruled what God placed inside of me. No matter what life threw at me, His value of me remained the same, what He saw in me remained the same; even though my perception about who He called me to be was a bit distorted. Yet, it still didn't cause God to change His mind about what He instilled inside me. No matter the poor decisions I made, God never changed his mind or decision about how He wanted to operate through me— His purpose for my life was SURE!

I know this now, but way back when I was in it... I couldn't see it. I was a mess. No matter what prayer line I went into the Word never changed. Seasons passed and things were getting better. I still battled with things, but I was getting stronger. I tried to be as consistent as I could possibly be. I knew I needed Jesus. The word came again about me carrying the fire of God in preparation for The Awakening Women's Encounter 2016.

This year we were prepping for the prophetic presbytery, and again Prophetess Carla was in our training, and again she released the prophetic Word about me carrying the fire of God. The Word of God wouldn't let me go. No matter how I tried to disqualify myself from it. The day of the Awakening Conference arrived, and everyone was excited. The excitement and expectation to see God's manifested power was so thick that you could cut it with a knife.

That year the theme was "Sound the Alarm". God came through and awakened each woman in attendance. The opening night, God's Word washed over us. We worshipped, we praised, and we prayed. Deliverance and healings were released! The next morning, the intercessors gathered for 6 AM morning glory prayer. As we were praying, Prophetess Carla made her way to me, and she began to release the Word of the Lord. But this time the Word was more detailed. *"Patrea, God is mantling you with the weight of His glory."* Prophetess Carla began to shift her weight onto me, and loudly exclaimed, *"The weight of God's GLORY"*. I had no clue as to what God was doing. I felt like the same old Patrea, but I was excited that he would mantle with such great honor. More prophetic words were released to me during the conference, and those words confirmed some of my private prayers, as well as other prophetic words that I received in other years.

I embraced them all, wrote them down, and stood on them. I was intentional about my purpose. So, this is where everything began to shift for me. A lot more transpired since the time of the 2016 Awakening conference, but this was when God spoke to me up close and personal.

I'm not sure what it was about these Awakening Reloaded encounters, but in 2017 the theme was "Stand Your Ground", and the guest speaker was Prophetess Tapika. God revealed Himself to me in a very real way! The woman of God spoke about breaking the ground, and the ground responding to our voice when we speak. God was drawing me in deeper and deeper with every Word this woman of God spoke, and before the benediction, an altar call ensued.

I felt led to go up, and the woman of God began to just sing this melodious *"o's"*. She sang them in different octaves. The *o's* were slow and steady—piercingly, intense yet powerful. She just walked the altar singing these *o's* back and forward she went.

I closed my eyes and just said desperately, *"Lord, speak to me. I want whatever you have for me. Lord, speak to me."* Suddenly, the room grew still, and the Holy Spirit softly told me to keep my eyes closed and wait. I kept my eyes closed, but I could feel myself drifting. I was still conscious of my surroundings, but it was like I was drifting to another place.

The *o's* of Prophetess Tapika seem to be coming closer, but it seemed like I was floating away. I was physically present —coherent, but my spirit and soul were in another place. I kept my eyes closed as instructed, never opened them. Now, the melodious *o's* where right in front of me. She never touched me, but I could feel the power of God surge through me. I fell to my knees. My eyes still closed tight. She continued to sing with more intensity. Then suddenly, out of the darkness, an image appeared. It was ME... This is the only way I can describe it to make sense. I was standing in the darkness with what looked like a ribbon of fire swirling around me, but the flames were in the shape of doves. It was quite perplexing, but I was intrigued, so I kept watching. At this point, I could no longer hear the singing. Everything around me was silent. But, I knew—I was in the presence of God.

God had taken me up into a place in the spirit. I focused on this 3D image that surrounded me with a swirling ribbon of fire. Then there was a flash of clips of me praying for and speaking to crowds of different women. I couldn't see their faces, but I could feel their presence in the room. I couldn't hear what I was saying, but I could see what I was doing. In the last clip, I was praying for a faceless woman. I couldn't see her face, but once I opened my mouth flames of fire came out and invisible chains began to fall off her, and each chain turned in to ashes. Then I heard the voice of the Lord say, *"you are My flame. You have been created to start fires in the earth."* I could slowly feel myself in the room once again, and at this point Pastor Nedra was speaking.

I was assisted from the floor, and in awe, I walked back to my seat. The vision flashed before my face, and I softly repeated the words *"I am the flame, I am the flame, I am the flame."* I didn't understand what I was speaking, but it resonated with my spirit. That night I went home told my husband and went straight into my prayer closet.

Every prophetic word spoken over me concerning fire flooded my mind. I committed each memory in time (2010, 2014, 2016) to detail. Never did I pursue those Words or looked into the Words spoken to me, but this night—I was intentional about finding out what God was saying. I sat quietly until finally, I said *God show me in Your Word what You are speaking to me. You said that I am the flame show me in your Word. I got to know that I'm hearing you correctly.*
Softly I heard, *"Hebrews 1:7"*.

I said Lord, *I don't understand?*

Again, softly the voice spoke, *"Hebrews 1:7"*.

I scurried, reaching for my Bible. Once it was in my hands, I was flipping through pages like a woman who had gone mad. Finally, the pages landed on Hebrews. Using my finger as a guide, I made it to verse seven that read, *"And of the angels He says: "Who makes His angels spirits and His ministers a flame of fire."*[82] I then crossed-referenced with Psalms 104:3-4 that reads, *"He lays the beams of His upper chambers in the waters, who makes the clouds His chariot, Who walks on the wings of the wind, who makes His angels spirits, His ministers a flame of fire."*[83]

I sat there amazed. I knew for sure that I had read these

scriptures before. How did I miss it? I praised God for revealing it in His Word to me. The Holy Spirit gentle spoke, *"You are His "Firestarter" you will ignite the hearts of many on the Father's behalf."* I was flooded with so many feelings I didn't know what to do. I told a few of the encounters but guarded some of the more sacred and personal conversations I had with the Holy Spirit. At that moment in my life, there was no more questioning. I knew what God had spoken to me. I didn't need to seek any further. God brought His Word to me. I would declare that Word over me every chance I got. Even when old think habits came back to try to torment me. I would speak the Word.

I went through all of that so you could see the battle I was fighting. Yes, I went through heartbreak. Yes, I went through disappointments and pain. Yes, I went through points of shame and embarrassment. Yes, I went through guilt. Victory, for me, didn't seem lasting. One day I was up, and the next I was down. I saw no hope for me. It seemed like change was impossible for me. My future looked bleak and obsolete.

But, through it, all God still called me His "Firestarter". I've received many prophetic words over the years, and I even saw and am still seeing the manifestation of them; but when I had that encounter with God concerning the "fire", life for me became different. I still had my struggles; everything didn't just go away, but over time I learned how to shift my weight in the spirit. I understood every battle was not mine to fight.

In 2018, I finally birthed the vision God place in my heart in 2015 called the A.W. E (Authentic Worship Empowerment) Summit. This summit broke me into a river of God-sustaining power. This summit was geared towards the intercessors, worship teams and leaders, dancers and dance leaders, and minstrels.

The A.W.E summit is a call to righteousness, healing, and deliverance for those fulfilling ministerial roles in leadership.

This summit served as an outlet for creatives in leadership to operate in our gifting free and whole. I was honored as this was my first time speaking for a service. I was terrified, but God had my back. He came in, and the people of God experienced the fire of God and received healing and deliverance.

Never allow the shame of your mistakes to forfeit the testimony of God's delivering power, never discount the little that you may have because God uses every situation you may go through to make HISTORY for you to share for someone else's BREAK OUT!

LET'S TALK FIRE—SHALL WE

Fire is an oxidizing chemical reaction that releases heat and light. The actual flames of fire that we see moving and glowing when something is burning is really a gas that's reacting and giving off light. Sounds like the Word of God to me. God's Word says that He is "*a lamp unto my feet, and a light unto my path.*[84] *God is a consuming fire.*[85] and it provides us with light.

Fire is also an important part of maintaining a diverse and healthy ecosystem. When fires burn in intervals it appropriates the ecosystem. When fire consumes leaf litter and other ground vegetation such as dead wood and twigs; it triggers a re-birthing of nature. Studies have shown that fire is one of nature's most essential agents of change.

How can we apply this information to us? Those who have been marked by fire have the ability to cultivate a diverse and healthy environment so that they can help others to birth out purpose. It is said that "fire" is nature's most essential agent of change. Well, I believe "Firestarters", are major change agents. I also believe just as natural fire can bring destruction; "Firestarters", can also wreak havoc and brings destruction on the kingdom of darkness. Fire is in a class all on its own. It doesn't have to seek attention, it doesn't have to ask to be noticed, and it JUST IS! It doesn't have to demand respect, but it commands it! What I've learned and what I'm still learning is that…

FIRE will test US…
"But on the judgment day, fire will reveal what kind of work each builder has done. The fire will show if a person's work has any value." This is why we can get so focused on the next person because our work is going to be put under fire. 1 Corinthians 3:13 NLT

FIRE Refines US…
"And it shall come to pass, that in all the land, saith the LORD, two parts therein shall be cut off and die; but the third shall be left therein. And I will bring the third part through the fire, and will refine them as silver is refined, and will try them as gold is tried: they shall call on my name, and I will hear them: I will say, It is my people: and they shall say, The LORD is my God.", Zechariah 13:8-9 King James Version (KJV)

FIRE WILL Purify US…
"He will sit as a refiner and purifier of silver, and he will purify the sons of Levi and refine them like gold and silver, and they will bring offerings in righteousness to the LORD." Malachi 3:3 ESV

FIRE WILL POSITION US AND Expose us…
"That the trial of your faith, being much more precious than of gold that perisheth, though it be tried with fire, might be found unto praise and honour and glory at the appearing of Jesus Christ." 1 Peter 1:7 (KJV)

Fire comes with EVIDENCE…

When something catches fire, there's evidence. You can feel the heat, see the flames, and smell the smoke. Fire is an undeniable substance, and it's hard to avoid. Fire can't be hidden.

It's always out in the open. At times there may be an unrecognizable flicker, and some may discount the flicker, but once enough oxygen is generated it will cause that flicker to set ablaze! Some of you may just be the flicker in need of someone who can fan the flames that will cause you to set communities on fire, companies on fire, and systems on fire!Don't negate your flicker. The flicker is just as important as the flame. The flicker is evidence that something has taken place and something is about to happen and can happen at any time. That's why it's important to know what you carry.

When you have a fire on the inside of you, it's evident. You don't have to go around telling everybody you have it because when you show up it's evident. When you open your mouth, it's evident. It is evident in your relationships. It's evident in your business endeavors. It's evident in your behavior and treatment of others because it's a part of your character.

Some of us have ignored the burning on the inside of us, and we have become complacent in our purpose, and our fire has dwindled. But I'm convinced that when we began to put your focus back on Jesus your "FIRE" WILL BE REIGNITED! The Bible declares that HE is a consuming fire, and I've found that if we get close enough to the fire then the heat will sustain us!

Do Not Despise the Little

If you were to meet me in person, you would instantly notice my small stature. This was one quality that I thought God missed. I despised being so small. I went through years of being bullied because I was so small. If I could just be a little taller then maybe the world around me would take me more serious—I thought. Everyone I encountered thought I was so much younger than I was, so often I would be overlooked and ignored.

As I grew older, I began to internalize all of the feelings about my height, weight, appearance, and shape. I outright despised everything about me, but I especially despised being so short. Everywhere I went people would comment on how I was so little, tiny, and skinny; whereas I was always thinking about how they were so tall, big, and fat. I started to allow my influence to be dictated by stature. Because I was so small, I also started to feel small. As a result, I dismissed and diminished my power and influence.

But as time went on I discovered that small things carry great power. I learned that there are small things that are worth fortunes. I'm telling you all of this because too often times we despise what we deem small as having little to no value. We despise our creativity, our uniqueness, our differences, and even our stories. Not understanding the impact and the influence that these things have on our lives and the lives of others, we begin to diminish some of our greatest gifts. We take our little and we just say to ourselves *"this is all I have to give."* In essence, we could live our life believing that. Taking all our gifts to the grave without experiencing the fullness of what those little gifts (little power, little influence, little smile, little joy, little hope, little conversation, or little oil) could do. Our little may be powerful enough to make HISTORY! YES. HISTORY!

Let me share a story in the Bible with you. It's a woman in that's noted of a widow. We don't know her name. All we know is that she was from a city named Zarephath, she was a widow, she had a son, and she was living in a famine. We are introduced to her after God tells Prophet Elijah to go to the city where she resides. We then learn that she is not only a mother and a widow, but we learn that she is selfless, trusting, grieving, and starving; yet she is focused. Read 1 Kings 17

Life for her was no crystal stair, but God considered her. She had nothing to offer no life to continue living; as a matter of fact, when the prophet entered the city's gate he found her gathering sticks to make her son and herself their last meal in preparation for their death.

Yes, she was done with life.

But, GOD...CONSIDERED...HER. The widow's miracle showed up on the scene, and the prophet's answer came from the little oil and flour in the flask of a widow premeditating her death at the gate. Her little made HISTORY. What am I saying in all of this...God considered a *nobody*! God used her little and multiplied it, and her little became the answer. Each of us are carrying something special.

Your little may be purposed to make a difference in the earth. Your little may establish governments or make blueprints. Your little may empower the hopeless and bring joy to the broken. Your little could be the solution to someone's problem right now. God considered the widow, and God considers you too.

Desperation will cause us to forfeit what we have in our possession. To protect our fire, we must understand what causes our fire to go extinguish. FIRESTARTERS ARE NOT ALLOWED TO JUST QUIT! Listen, When God marks us to do something great, it's not always going to be a bed of roses. However, it still requires our obedience, discipline, commitment, and an uncompromising YES! When God impregnates us with something of great value please understand it will come with a cost, but a cost that's well worth it. A cost that causes us to make History.

You've been marked with something exceptional. You can't get rid of it, and it just won't let you go. You're carrying something magnificent, and you know it! It makes you stay when you want to run away, it makes you pray when you want to stop. YOU ARE CARRYING SOMETHING SPECIAL, AND NOW IT'S BEING TESTED! Don't abort the assignment YOU WERE MARKED FOR THIS!

Considered to Make History

History is an established record of a past that is notable

for its important unusual, or interesting event. We have history, but God wants us to capture the unusual and interesting events of our lives that would bring Him glory and set the captives free. I want you to take note of the fact that God chose the widow. We don't even know her name, we don't even know where she originally came from—we know nothing of her background, but yet God decided to incorporate and highlight that moment in time. The Widow's gift is a history that has/will influence the people of faith and others throughout eternity. God chose her! Not only to restore her life but to declare through her that He is the He is the Resurrection of Life. To witness firsthand that He was/is the Giver of Life! She was the first to see the resurrecting power of God. (Continue to Read 1 Kings 17 Chapter)

God had already chosen her for that moment in time, even though she was going through the worst part of her life. God chose to highlight her in the midst of her pain, her grief, her sorrow, and her anguish. He chose to shine the light on her frailty and her low state. She was not polished or pristine. She was not quoting scriptures and speaking in tongues. Quite the contrary, she was preparing for her death.

However, God looked down into the earth and selected this weakened, broken, and unknown lady for a monumental moment that would impact the timeline of history forever. We see that her purpose goes far beyond her suffering. What am I trying to say here? We are not exempted from pain. During this very moment, you may be dealing with something heavy. You may feel like you have nothing left but a little oil in your jar of hope. But, can I tell you this? God will take that pain and turn it into VICTORY, and then turn that victory into HISTORY with your little oil. God will take your little oil and set somethings in motion in the earth. God uses the unlikeliest things in our lives that will in turn cause others around us to live, thrive, and grow. Don't discount what you've been through or what you may be going through.

You see the widow was an answer. She was the instrument—a permanent fixture in Prophet Elijah's life and ministry. She was historical. You see, God will often ask us to offer up the little we have left so that He can do greater with it than our little minds could even fathom. Not only does he choose us, he prepares us, and we are unknowing. In verse 9 of 1 Kings 17, the Lord tells Elijah that he has commanded a widow woman to sustain him. So, before the widow even showed up on the scene, God selected her. How long do you think God was preparing her? How long had she known what would be asked of her in the coming days of Elijah? Not only was she the answer—her answer showed up, and she was open to receive revelation from the Lord, and her obedience set something supernatural in motion even during her hardest of circumstances.

She didn't have a clue that God had chosen to shine the spotlight on life on her, but God had already chosen her to be a part of something more wonderful than anything her brokenness could ever imagine. Like the widow, you to have been hand-picked by a Creator who knew you before you even came about. He created you to be a history maker. You were born to start fires. From this day forth never discount the little you may have. Your little oil just may cause you to be a firsthand witness to God's miracle-working power.

It's time for you to work with what you have. Let your flicker turn into a flame. Your flicker will provide strength to the weary. Remember who you are. Remember whose you are. Refuse to lay down and die. You are carrying something special. Don't let your faith die, don't let your hope die, don't let your heart wax cold. Don't let life change your confession, don't let the world put out your flame.

You might be saying, *"Patrea you don't understand. I can't take it anymore. I don't have anything left to give. I am depleted, and I feel downright defeated. It feels like I'm in a vicious cycle with no escape*. Well, this Firestarter has come to remind you that you have what it takes. Your feelings can't be trusted. Your purpose is certain, and your destiny is secure. You are in the right place and the right season for God to allow you to make HISTORY!

When we come to the end of ourselves that is when God does the supernatural in our lives. That's when God shows up and exceeds our expectations, thus putting us in awe of Him. Begin to ask God to ignite your fire. God is FAITHFUL! God is CAPABLE, God is ABLE and WILLING to set you ABLAZE! He is the God of Isaac, Abraham, and JACOB!

We talked about the widow and the gift of life, but what about those whose background and environment developed them to be outlandish? Those who were birthed into chaos and dishonesty? How can God possibly concern this disheveled ME?

Well, I say to you, "GOD IS STILL GOD, EVEN IN THE MIST OF CHAOS! GOD IS STILL GOD, EVEN WHEN WE HAVE IT ALTOGETHER, AND HE'S STILL GOD WHEN IT SEEMS LIKE EVERYTHING IS FALLING APART AROUND US! GOD IS STILL GOD, EVEN WE HAVE A FLICKER, AND HE'S STILL GOD WHEN OUR HEARTS ARE SET ABLAZE! GOD IS THE GOD WHO CALLED YOU! CHOSE YOU! PREDESTINATED YOU! WHO CALLS YOU BY NAME, AND WHO MARKED YOU BY FIRE! HE SELECTED YOU! GOD IS STILL GOD, AND HE IS STILL IN CONTROL".

What we've done in the past and even what we battle within the present; did not catch God by surprise. No matter how much you try to disqualify yourself. God never will change His mind about you. You heard some of my story. I tried to sabotage everything God called me to do. I thought I could fade into the background and gradually disappear. But, fire glows brightest in the dark. No matter how dark it gets, the Fire of God will expose you. Now, instead of running, I go low, so He can go high. "Not because I'm so great, but the One who lives in me makes me GREAT." He considered me and He considers you. Right now!

Right at this moment, God has been preparing you. He considers everything about you. You are the chosen. No one in your family has done what you are about to do. As a matter of fact, it's never been seen before. You were born for this! You were born to blaze trails, set fires, and consume generations for Christ! You were born MARKED!

Tell your past that it can no longer confine you because you have been marked by fire. Tell your mistakes that they don't define you because you have been marked by fire. Command that pain to break of you and burn by FIRE! Command that fear and anxiety to get off you and die by FIRE! DECLARE IN THE ATMOSPHERE, "I'M NOT WHAT HAS HAPPENED TO ME"!

The metaphysical meaning of Zarephath (Hebrew)-place of refinement; smelter; smelting place; place of purification with fire; place of purity; place of trial. Meta. The purifying fires of the inner subjective life centers. Jesus! Did you see that...Zarephath is a place of refinement? Why? Refinement is a process of removing unwanted elements. Don't despite the little...

God came in and shook up her world. He provided life, and He worked a miracle for a no-named widow. He refined, shaped, and marked with fire a nameless widow. He chose this nameless widow to make history. So, if He could do it for her, then He will do it for you too! Come on ask God to shakes up your world. Ask God to refine you. Tell Him that He can make you a history maker. Tell Him that He can use your pain to save souls. Tell Him that He can use your story to display His glory. Tell God to cause your flicker to be set ablaze. God has marked a remnant of believers in this hour to be history makers. You were born to start fires, and you were marked by fire to create History!

(SPEAK IT OUT LOUD)

AFFIRMATION: Chosen

I am chosen. I am qualified. I have been hand-picked by the Hand of God. He called me out of the darkness and brought me into His marvelous light. He shaped me, refined me, formed me, and marked me with His fire. I bask in my peculiarity. I love my differences. I love my calm. I love my cool, and I'm in love with my uniqueness. My failures don't define me. My mistakes can't make me fold. I have been chosen. Yes, touched by the finger of the Almighty God. He knows my name. He defines me. He accepts me. He washes me. He decided and considered me.

I choose to agree with God's decision concerning me. I choose to agree with what He says about me. He orchestrated my purpose. He fashioned my gifts, my wit, and my uniqueness. So, I choose to embody it. I will protect it, and I cover it with the Word of God.

I am chosen; not because I'm so great own my own, but God has given me the shield of His salvation, and His right hand holds me up, and His gentleness makes me great.[86] I'm chosen, because God chose me. God has chosen me to come to Him, and He has call me, He has given me the right standing with Him, and has given me His glory.[87] He decided. So, I accept it. Today, I come into agreement with the fact that I have been hand selected, set aside; to make history. I am a HISTORY MAKER-- MARKED BY FIRE for such a time as this.

Restored Fire

Throughout these chapters, I have shared my pain and my victories. Pain has its purpose, and God has a way of using that pain to our advantage. Although I have had some suffering, I praise God for them all. My pain reminds me of my God-given victory. He restored my soul, and He made me whole. God is still working some things out in me and causing me to grow stronger each day. When I tell you; there nothing like being restored! None of my old relationships are the same, and I am grateful for that! Pastor Sarah Jakes Roberts puts it this way, *"Just because the good thing in our lives had to die; doesn't mean that we lose our purpose and destiny."*

I had to lose some things so that I could see God from a healthier perspective. I had to lose some things so that when he restored me with new friendships and new divine relationships, I would know how to better handle them. Sometimes we have to lose to win. Sometimes we have to let go of the very thing that we hold near and dear to us so that we can receive and be everything God has purposed us to be. I'm still healing for some deep soul wounds, but it doesn't change the fact that God has marked me. I've chosen to forgive those who have hurt me, abandoned me, and I've stepped back to allow God to deal with their hearts.

However, overall, I understand now that it was never about the people anyway. It was all based on my response to the call of God on my life. Yes, you see God used each person as an instrument to put me in the correct posture me. And...Yes, of course. I endured some hurtful situations, and I've caused grief and done some hurtful things to others as well. But...the focal point of the journey throughout this book was not necessarily the pain or the disappointment, but how to overcome it, and how to help others maneuver through their pain in order to fulfill their God-given purpose on their lives.

Too often we look at the lives of others, and it appears as if they have no struggles, no woes of life, but on the contrary we all do. Hopefully, you can look at my woes of life and learn that trouble don't last always and that my life has been a testament of God's grace. I hope that you can look at all of my poor decisions, my pain, and tell yourself that if she was able to overcome all of that and press through—I can too.

What I have gained from it all—is how to own my stuff. When you can own your own STUFF (the good, the bad, and the ugly). You will be able to move through the processes of life without restrictions, embarrassments, or setbacks. Why? Because you will be able to navigate through your stuff and identify the things that get you out of position. When you take ownership of your stuff in essence you are taking responsibility for your actions, your behaviors, and how you handle the things that life throws your way. It's a good thing.

Listen, I didn't want to always want to own my STUFF, and life for me hadn't always been a bed of rose, but what I can tell you that I wouldn't change a thing. Remember, God uses everything. Every battle, every failure, every mishap, every victory, every point of growth, every part of our lives! Whoever said being marked would be easy?! When we hear the term "marked" we somehow think right away it's this amazing thing that doesn't come with a cost. But believe me...everything comes with a cost, even when we are unaware of the price.

Let me tell you. I struggled with this reality for a while. I even questioned God, "why me"? But why not me, why not you?! Listen, God is restoring me; and has restored some places in me that I refuse to revisit. God will do the same for you too. You can't blaze trials if you won't stop looking in the review of your past. The past is just that the past. The only time you such reach back in the past is for reminders of how much you have grown! Like a said before, "Whoever said being marked was going to be easy?!"

Fire requires heat. So, don't be afraid of the FIRE. DON'T YOU RUN AWAY FROM THE HEAT! The fire was/is necessary for the shaping. The heat was/is necessary for the molding! When it's all said and done... You will look up and find yourself right in the place God has purposed you to be—doing the things you were purposed and created to do! ON FIRE AND SET ABLAZE—MARKED BY FIRE AND MAKING HISTORY!

MOMENTS OF EMPOWERMENT

Affirmations

I hope that you enjoy these extracted affirmations from my *Be Bold Empowerment* Journal. As I stated in earlier pages of this book, I believe in the power of affirmations. Why do I believe in them so much— you ask? Well, because affirmations enable us to affirm some things about us, and when we speak them into the atmosphere; the manifestation of the things in which we speak begins to shape our thoughts, govern our feels, and redirect our focus.

To affirm means to state as a fact; assert strongly and publicly. It is our strong public declaration and self-reminders of facts that God has established in heaven and Earth about us! It's who we are! When we being to affirm what heaven has said about us OH MY GOSH, we begin to set things in motions by the power of our words!

Let me share a quote with you on a blog that I came across by Sean Gordon. I really love it! It says, "I am. Two of the most powerful words; for what you put after them shapes your reality."[88]

This quote is sobering. Think about what you speak out loud and also what you speak inwardly. What "I am's" are you speaking? What reality are you shaping with your words? Words are powerful! Look at what God did in Genesis 1:3, *"Then God said, "Let there be light"; and there was light."* God used His words to shape and to bring into existence His desired results. We have that same power on the inside of us to create with our words, because we have been created in the image of God to do so. See Genesis 1:27. Also, we are told in scripture, *"that death and life are in the power of the tongue, and those who love it will eat its fruit."* Proverbs 18:21 (NKJV)[89]

Speaking the proper words will give us life and establish our faith. So you have to speak it and to you see it. Speak it until you become it. You are what You Think. You are what you speak. Speak well, HISTORY MAKER!

AFFIRMATION OF LOVE

I am loved with an everlasting love.

I am worthy of love and deserve to receive love in abundance. I am perfected in love and fear has no place in my heart or my life. I will pursue love and continue in love. Love is my portion. God has lavished me with a love so great that He calls me his own.

I PUT OFF and I PUT ON

Because I am loved, I walk in love. I put off everything that causes me to lack in love. I put off bitterness, envy, jealousy, and strife; and I put on the love of Christ according to John 15:12.

AFFIRMATION OF STRENGTH

I am strengthened through Christ Jesus, and I can do all things.

I have strength to conquer anything that comes my way.

I am a vessel God uses; to strengthen, encourage, and comfort others.

I am clothed with strength and with favor.

I PUT OFF and I PUT ON

Today I have been strengthened to put off any/everything that will cause me to be derailed in my faith, and to be weakened in my belief system. I put off the lack of strength now in the name of Jesus Christ, and I put on the strength of the Lord that will allow me to tread in high places to Habakkuk 3:19.

AFFIRMATION OF POWER

I am clothed in power, might, and strength; I can't be stopped. I have been given divine power; I have everything that pertains to life and godliness.

I am a child of God, and I believe that He is able to do exceedingly and abundantly above all that I can ask or think according to the power that works through me.

I am Holy Spirit-filled; and the Spirit of the Lord is upon me and I He's given me POWER.

I have power and my weapons of warfare are not carnal, but mighty through God to pull down and destroy strongholds.

I PUT OFF and I PUT ON

I have been given the power to overcome the enemy, and I put off any/everything that will cause me to be frail and weakened in who God has called me to be. I put off brokenness and frailty now in the name of Jesus Christ, and I put on the power of the Holy Spirit that causes me to triumph over the enemy according to Luke 10:19.

AFFIRMATION OF VICTORY

I am victorious—there is nothing that I cannot overcome. I triumph in victory through Christ Jesus, and I am thankful. I am a child of God walking in power and consistent victory. I am spirit-filled and sickness and diseases are far from me.

I am more than a conquer through Christ Jesus.

I PUT OFF and I PUT ON

I am victorious in the Lord, for my God has given me the power to tread on serpents and scorpions, and over all the power of the enemy, and nothing shall by any means hurt me. I come out of agreement with any/everything that will cause me to operate in failure or defeat. I put off a defeated mindset now in the name of Jesus Christ, and I put on triumphant victory according to 1 Corinthians 15:57.

AFFIRMATION OF FREEDOM

I am free from guilt, shame, and condemnation.

I am set free, I am set apart, and free from condemnation. I have been called out of darkness into God's marvelous light.

I am free through Christ Jesus.

I am a new creation in Christ, and old things have passed away, and all things for me are new.

I PUT OFF and I PUT ON

I am free to be who God has created me to be. My liberty is not predicated based on my past failures, my past mistakes, or shortcomings. My freedom is not based on the opinions of others. I come out of agreement with any/everything that will try with desperate attempts to get me entangled with old habits, behaviors, and thinking again. I put off the spirit of bondage now in the name of Jesus Christ and I put on freedom according to Galatians 5:1.

AFFIRMATION OF FAVOR

I am favored, appreciated, and God knows my name.

I have favor with God and with man.

My gifts are making room for me and placing me before great people.

I am daily loaded with benefits. What it will take other years to do—I will learn in a matter of weeks. I am the apple of God's eye and he favors me.

I PUT OFF and I PUT ON

Today, I embrace the favor that rests on my life. I refuse to agree with any/everything that will try to get me to believe that I can't afford what life has to offer me. I put off disapproval now in the name of Jesus Christ and I put on the favor of God according to Psalm 5:12.

AFFIRMATION OF RIGHTEOUSNESS

I am the righteousness in Christ Jesus, and I can run into Him and I am saved.

I am made righteous through the blood of my savior Jesus Christ.

I am justified by my faith; completely forgiven and made righteous through Christ. Because I am righteous; my prayers are heard and avail much.

I PUT OFF and I PUT ON

Today, I am settled in who God has called me to be, and I can have the confessions in which I speak because I believe. I cut myself out of agreement with any/everything that says that I'm other than what God says about me. I put off false humility now in the name of Jesus Christ and I put on the spirit of righteousness according to Job 29:14.

AFFIRMATION OF IDENTITY

I am beautifully, uniquely, and wonderfully made.

I am one of a kind…there is no one like me ever.

I am something special, something magnificent, something exuberant, and powerful.

I am the craftsmanship of the Almighty Creator.

I PUT OFF and I PUT ON

There is only one of me, and I have been designed for a purpose. I am it! I can impact the world with who/what I am. I fully accept this fact as my truth. I come out of agreement with any/everything that does not line up with this truth. I put off all identity crises now in the name of Jesus Christ and I put on my identity in Christ in whom I live according to Galatians 2:20.

AFFIRMATION OF PEACE

I have the mind of Christ; peace is my portion.

I am perfected in love, I have power, and I have a sound mind. My mind is focused on things that are true, honest, just, pure, lovely, and of good report.

I have a mind that stays on Jesus, and He keeps me in perfect peace.

I am a peacemaker, and I am called a child of God.

I PUT OFF and I PUT ON

Today, I refuse to let life's situations rattle or shake me. I come out of agreement with any/everything that will try to rob me of my peace. I put off contention now in the name of Jesus Christ, and I put on the peace and turn away from evil according to Psalm 34:4.

AFFIRMATION OF HEALING

I am healed and spirit-filled sickness and disease are far from me.

I have been forgiven from all inequities, and I have been healed from all diseases.

My body is healthy, my heart is strong, and my emotions are healed.

I am willing and able to receive my healing. By the stripes of Jesus, I am healed completely.

I PUT OFF and I PUT ON

Today, I come out of agreement with any/everything that comes against the truth of God's Word concerning my healing. I put off brokenness, sickness, and disease now in the name of Jesus Christ, and I put on the power of healing, and when I cry out to the Lord he will send word and heal me according to Psalm 30:2.

AFFIRMATION OF ACCEPTANCE

I am loved and accepted by God and by man.

I have been accepted into the beloved of God.

I am justified, qualified, approved of, and called by God.

I am the apple of God's eye…and He loves me completely.

I am a child of God and born of an incorruptible seed of the Word of God (Jesus).

I PUT OFF and I PUT ON

Today, I step into my rightful place as a daughter of the Most High. I come out of agreement with any/everything that says that I'm not wanted, desired, or accepted. I put off rejection now in the name of Jesus Christ and I put on the spirit of adoption according to Ephesians 1:5-7.

AFFIRMATION OVER THE MIND

I have the mind of Christ.

I have a sound mind, and clarity of thought.

I am capable of making the right decisions.

My mind is healed, freed, and sound.

I PUT OFF and I PUT ON

Today, I come out of agreement with any/everything that comes against the truth of God's Word concerning my healing. I put off brokenness, sickness, and disease now in the name of Jesus Christ and I put on the power of healing and when I cry out to the Lord he will send word and heal me according to Psalm 30:2

AFFIRMATION OF OBEDIENCE

I am willing and obedient, and I will eat the fruit of the land.

I am a doer of the word and not only a hearer.

I love the Lord, and I will obey His teachings.

I fully obey the Lord my God and carefully follow His instructions.

I walk in full obedience to all that the Lord speaks to me so that I will live, prosper, and have prolonged days as I possess the promises of the Lord.

I PUT OFF and I PUT ON

I love the Lord with all my heart, mind, and soul; so, I will obey Him. I refuse and refute any/everything that will try to pull me away from being obedient to the will of God. I put off disobedience now in the name of Jesus Christ and I put on the spirit of obedience and God will set me above all the nations of the earth according to Deuteronomy 28:1.

AFFIRMATION OVER THE HEART

I have a pure heart that loves the Lord.

My heart is pure before God and he hears me when I call.

I have clean hands and a pure heart.

I am buried with Christ, and dead to the power of sin's rule over my life.

I hide the Word of the Lord in my heart so that I will not sin against my Heavenly Father.

I PUT OFF and I PUT ON

Today, I make a covenant with myself to always protect and guard my heart against all things that don't align with the Word,

Will, and Way of God. I refute and disallow any/everything that will try full my heart with hatred, bitterness, fear, doubt, or disobedience. I put off hard-heartedness now in the name of Jesus Christ, and I put on a new heart of flesh according to Ezekiel 36:26.

AFFIRMATION OF FAITH

I am a woman of FAITH.

I have an unshakeable faith that moves mountains.

I am justified by faith, and I have peace with God through Christ Jesus.

I have the now faith. It is the substance of the things that I hope for, and the evidence not seen. My faith is strengthened because I incline my ears to hear the Word of God.

I PUT OFF and I PUT ON

I am secure in my faith and will not be shaken by what life throws my way. I refuse and refute any/everything that will try to shake my faith. I put off fear now in the name of Jesus Christ; and I put on faith, increase in faith, and I will live by faith according to Romans 1:17.

AFFIRMATION OF THE WORD

The Word of the Lord dwells richly on the inside of me.

I am filled with the Word of God. I am sustained by the Word of God. I am rooted, anchored, and tied to the Word of God. I am hidden in the Word of God.

I PUT OFF and I PUT ON

The Word of the Lord is a light unto my feet and a lamp unto my path. I will reject any/everything that will try to turn me away from the truth of God's Word and. I put off ignorance now in the name of Jesus Christ, and I put on the truth of God's Word according to Proverbs 30:5.

AFFIRMATION OF BLESSINGS

I am blessed in the city and blessed in the field.

My life is blessed. I am daily loaded with heavenly blessings. Everything connected to me is blessed.

I am ridiculously blessed...my blessings chase me down and overtake me.

I PUT OFF and I PUT ON

Today, I will shout it from the rooftop that I am blessed, fortunate, and graced with many blessings. I disallow and veto any/everything that will rob me of my blessings. I put off lack now in the name of Jesus Christ, and I put on the spirit of abundance according to Deuteronomy 30:9.

AFFIRMATION OF BOLDNESS

I am bold and can access BIG rooms with confidence through my faith in Christ Jesus. I am willing, able, and capable to speak with boldness. I am adaptable, confident, influential, and bold. I am enthusiastic, fervent, assertive, positive, and ever-increasing with ease and magnitude prolonged life and renewed strength. I am bold as a lion, and I will possess the promises of God fearlessly.

I PUT OFF and I PUT ON

I am who I am. Unapologetically, undeniably, and undauntedly ME. I denounce and renounce any/everything that will try to strip me of boldness. I put off fear now in the name of Jesus Christ, and I put on boldness and courage according to Joshua 1:9.

About the Author

Patrea Brumfield is a dynamic and vivacious personality who empowers, motivates, and inspires others to be the very best version of themselves that God has designed them to be. Patrea uses her experiences and relatable situations to encourage, reignite, redefine, and reshape the thoughts of others. Her testimonies enable others to view life from a new perspective by activating them to live life fully, freely, unapologetically, and uncompromisingly.

Patrea has an uncanny ability to connect with people through her straightforward, animated, and sincere sense of humor. In addition to exposing her victories, she plainly reveals some of the massive challenges she has faced throughout her life's journey, and more importantly, she shares how she overcame and grew from them. Her message of BOLDNESS is what fuels her passion to help others break out of the box of complacency into investigating and discovering their true identity in Christ Jesus; thus, expanding and advancing the Kingdom of God. She is truly a yielded vessel who lives a sacrificial life before the Lord so that through her transparency, she can encourage others to be drawn closer to the Father.

www.patreabrumfield.com

Acknowledgments

To my loving husband William Brumfield, thank you for hanging in there during the most turbulent years of my life. It's because of your love, support, and prayers that I was able to embrace the fire of God. I love you with my entire being. You make my life complete. Thank you, babe, for everything you do. I wouldn't want to do this thing called "LIFE" without you. Me and You against the world.

To my precious boys: Jeremiah Brumfield and William Brumfield, III. I love and adore you two. You mean the world to me. I would give my life for you both at a drop of a hat. Every day I choose to be better because I want you both to always see better and do better. I want to be that example to make you both go after everything God places into your hearts. Thank you both for loving me even during moments when I was not as loving as I should have been while discovering who God has purposed me to be. It's a must that generational curses must be broken so that functional living is restored. The Brumfields' have been MARKED by FIRE, and we are destined to make history. Sometimes love can look different when our hearts and souls have been wounded, but God is faithful to restore. I love each of you with all my heart, and I mean it.

To my sisters, Reatee Freeman and Brittany Sims. I do what I do to show you that you can too. You two are my motivation. I want my niece and nephews to see their mothers walking free, fulfilling purpose, and being free and heal. Thank you for your constant support and encouraging words. I love you, two knuckleheads.

To my daddy, Victor Freeman. Words can't express the magnitude of love I have for you. You've taught me so much. I love the way I love because of you. You taught me to know strength, loyalty, fidelity, honesty, and integrity. Thank you for your unfailing love for me. Always a daddy's girl. Thank you for being my daddy.

To my Mama, LaDona Faye. Thank you for being the vessel God used to birth purpose into the earth. Every day I wonder how life would be if I had you here with me. I hope that I've made you proud. Love you always. Rest in heaven.

I would like to acknowledge Pastor Toemeika Goard, who I affectionately call my spiritual auntie. It is because of your obedience that this book has been entitled *Marked by Fire*. The Word of the Lord you spoke over me in 2018 remained hidden in my heart. Thank you for encouraging me to share the fire. Love you always

To my Sister-Friend Jennifer Gray, you have been an essential part of the process of me completing this book. Thank you for your love, your support, your encouragement, your accountability, and your unfailing prayer. I love you. We are forever bonded by prayer. Prayer Purpose Sisters. Your friendship came at a time when I needed it most. God allowed you to be my fresh start. Thank you.

To Pastor Nedra Buckmire, I love you! My goodness! Thank you for being my inspiration of HOPE from near and from afar. Your constant encouragement throughout the years helped me to hope again. You never ceased to remind me of who God called me to be even during my low moments. I still hold on to the prophetic word given to me from Prophetess Carla back in 2011. I'm sure you know what I'm talking about because I remind you every chance I get. Thank you so much for your love.

Be B.O.L.D

Resources
Be Bold Empowerment Journal
Be Bold Women's Empowerment Conference
Be Bold Empowerment Life Coaching
A Journey From Brokenness To Boldness
8-Week Mentorin g Program
Break Out: An Excursion To Freedom
6-Week Coaching Program

Upcoming Titles
Cover Me BOLD Affirmations, Prayers, and Declarations that Release Power- (2021)

If this book was useful to you, why not share it with your leaders and friends? Take a moment to leave a review on Amazon and on my website so that others can make history!

References

[1] New Living Translation Bible

[2] Psalm 139:13 King James Version

[3] Psalm 119:73 King James Version

[4] Merriam-Webster Dictionary

[5] Google Dictionary

[6] New King James Version
[7] New King James Version
[8] New King James Version Bible
[9] New King James Version

[10] Matthew 21-28 New King James Version

[11] Google Dictionary

[12] 1 John 3:8 King James Version (KJV)

[13] King James Version Bible

[14] King James Version Bible

[15] New King James Version Bible

[16] New King James Version Bible

[17] Vocabulary.com

[18] Wikipedia-en.wikipedia.org

[19] King James Version Bible

[20] King James Version Bible

[21] New King James Version Bible

[22] Philippians 2:12 New King James Version Bible

[23] Matthew 17:21 New King James Version Bible

[24] John Bereve, The Bait of Satan, 2014

[25] Cambridge Dictionary

[26] Merriam-Webster Dictionary
[27] New King James Bible
[28] Hebrews 11:6 New King James Version Bible
[29] New King James Version Bible
[30] New King James Version Bible
[31] New King James Version
[32] New King James Version Bible
[33] New King James Version Bible
[34] New King James Version Bible
[35] New King James Version Bible
[36] New King James Version Bible
[37] New King James Version
[38] https://soulsurvivorworship.com/blog/worship-is-a-weapon
[39] https://soulsurvivorworship.com/blog/worship-is-a-weapon
[40] New King James Version Bible
[41] James 4:7 New Kings James Version Bible
[42] James 4:8 New Kings James Version Bible
[43] New King James Version
[44] New King James Version Bible
[45] King James Version Bible
[46] King James Version Bible
[47] Google Dictionary
[48] Collins Online Dictionary
[49] New King James Version Bible
[50] New King James Version Bible
[51] New King James Version Bible
[52] New King James Version Bible
[53] New King James Version Bible
[54] Google Dictionary
[55] Google Dictionary
[56] Psalm 139:14 King James Version
[57] New King James Version
[58] New King James Version Bible
[59] New King James Version Bible

[60] Blueletterbible.org

[61] New King James Version Bible

[62] Blueletterbibe.org

[63] New King James Version Bible

[64] New King James Version Bible

[65] New King James Version Bible

[66] Google Dictionary

[67] Merriam Webster Dictionary

[68] Merriam Webster Dictionary

[69] http://www.truthunity.net/mbd/lo-debar

[70] http://www.truthunity.net/mbd/lo-debar

[71] New King James Version (NKJV)

[72] New King James Version (NKJV)

[73] New King James Version (NKJV)

[74] New King James Version (NKJV)

[75] Dictionary.com

[76] New King James Version

[77] 2 Corinthians 11:14

[78] Dictionary.com

[79] John 8:32

[80] Dictionary.com

[81] New King James Version Bible

[82] Hebrews 1:7 New King James Version

[83] Psalms 104:3-4 New King James Version

[84] Psalm 119:105 New King James Version Bible

[85] Hebrews 12:29 New King James Version Bible

[86] Psalms 18:35 New King James Version

[87] Romans 8:30 New Living Translation NLT

[88] www.seangordon.com.au

[89] New Kings James Version Bible

Made in the USA
Coppell, TX
17 February 2022